1 AND 2 CORINTHIANS

FORTRESS COMMENTARY ON THE BIBLE

Fortress Commentary on the Bible: The Old Testament and Apocrypha
Fortress Commentary on the Bible: The New Testament
The Pentateuch: Fortress Commentary on the Bible Study Edition
The Prophets: Fortress Commentary on the Bible Study Edition
Wisdom, Worship, and Poetry: Fortress Commentary on the Bible Study Edition
The Historical Writings: Fortress Commentary on the Bible Study Edition
The Gospels and Acts: Fortress Commentary on the Bible Study Edition
The Letters and Legacy of Paul: Fortress Commentary on the Bible Study Edition
Hebrews, the General Epistles, and Revelation: Fortress Commentary on the Bible Study Edition
1 and 2 Kings: Fortress Commentary on the Bible
Isaiah: Fortress Commentary on the Bible
Mark: Fortress Commentary on the Bible
1 and 2 Corinthians: Fortress Commentary on the Bible

1 AND 2 CORINTHIANS

FORTRESS COMMENTARY ON THE BIBLE

LAURA NASRALLAH
DAVID E. FREDRICKSON

FORTRESS PRESS
Minneapolis

1 AND 2 CORINTHIANS
Fortress Commentary on the Bible

31 30 29 28 27 26 25 1 2 3 4 5 6 7 8 9

Library of Congress Control Number: 2025035436 (print)

Cover design: Kris E. Miller
Cover image: compilation of stock textures from Getty Images

Print ISBN: 979-8-3419-0015-8
eBook ISBN: 979-8-3419-0016-5

CONTENTS

CONTRIBUTORS

Laura Nasrallah
Professor of New Testament Criticism and Interpretation
Yale Divinity School

David E. Fredrickson
Professor of New Testament
Luther Seminary

Volume Editors

Margaret Aymer
Associate Professor of New Testament and Chair of Biblical Studies
Interdenominational Theological Center

Cynthia Briggs Kittredge
Dean and President and Professor of New Testament
Seminary of the Southwest

David A. Sánchez
Associate Professor of Theological Studies
Loyola Marymount University

ABBREVIATIONS

General

AT	Alpha Text (of the Greek text of Esther)
BOI	Book of Isaiah
Chr	Chronicler
DH	Deuteronomistic History
DI	Deutero-Isaiah
Dtr	Deuteronomist
Gk.	Greek
H	Holiness Code
Heb.	Hebrew
JPS	Jewish Publication Society
LXX	The Septuagint
LXX B	Vaticanus Text of the Septuagint
MP	Mode of production
MT	Masoretic Text
NIV	New International Version
NRSV	New Revised Standard Version
OAN	Oracles against Nations (in Jeremiah)
P.	papyrus/papyri
P	Priestly source
PE	Pastoral Epistles
RSV	Revised Standard Version
TI	Trito-Isaiah

Books of the Bible (NT, OT, Apocrypha)

Old Testament/Hebrew Bible

Gen.	Genesis
Exod.	Exodus
Lev.	Leviticus
Num.	Numbers
Deut.	Deuteronomy
Josh.	Joshua
Judg.	Judges
Ruth	Ruth
1 Sam.	1 Samuel
2 Sam.	2 Samuel
1 Kgs.	1 Kings
2 Kgs.	2 Kings
1 Chron.	1 Chronicles
2 Chron.	2 Chronicles
Ezra	Ezra
Neh.	Nehemiah
Esther	Esther
Job	Job
Ps. (Pss.)	Psalms
Prov.	Proverbs
Eccles.	Ecclesiastes
Song.	Song of Songs
Isa.	Isaiah
Jer.	Jeremiah
Lam.	Lamentations
Ezek.	Ezekiel
Dan.	Daniel
Hosea	Hosea
Joel	Joel
Amos	Amos
Obad.	Obadiah
Jon.	Jonah
Mic.	Micah
Nah.	Nahum
Hab.	Habakkuk

Zeph.	Zephaniah
Hag.	Haggai
Zech.	Zechariah
Mal.	Malachi

Apocrypha

Tob.	Tobit
Jth.	Judith
Gk. Esther	Greek Additions to Esther
Sir.	Sirach (Ecclesiasticus)
Bar.	Baruch
Let. Jer.	Letter of Jeremiah
Add Dan.	Additions to Daniel
Pr. Azar.	Prayer of Azariah
Sg. Three.	Song of the Three Young Men (or Three Jews)
Sus.	Susanna
Bel	Bel and the Dragon
1 Macc.	1 Maccabees
2 Macc.	2 Maccabees
1 Esd.	1 Esdras
Pr. of Man.	Prayer of Manasseh
2 Esd.	2 Esdras
Wis.	Wisdom of Solomon
3 Macc.	3 Maccabees
4 Macc.	4 Maccabees

New Testament

Matt.	Matthew
Mark	Mark
Luke	Luke
John	John
Acts	Acts of the Apostles
Rom.	Romans
1 Cor.	1 Corinthians
2 Cor.	2 Corinthians
Gal.	Galatians

Eph.	Ephesians
Phil.	Philippians
Col.	Colossians
1 Thess.	1 Thessalonians
2 Thess.	2 Thessalonians
1 Tim.	1 Timothy
2 Tim.	2 Timothy
Titus	Titus
Philem.	Philemon
Heb.	Hebrews
James	James
1 Pet.	1 Peter
2 Pet.	2 Peter
1 John	1 John
2 John	2 John
3 John	3 John
Jude	Jude
Rev.	Revelation (Apocalypse)

Journals, Series, Reference Works

ANF	*The Ante-Nicene Fathers*. Edited by Alexander Roberts and James Donaldson. 1885–1887. 10 vols. Repr., Peabody, MA: Hendrickson, 1994.
ANTC	Abingdon New Testament Commentaries
A(Y)B	Anchor (Yale) Bible
CBQMS	Catholic Biblical Quarterly Monograph Series
HNTC	Harper's New Testament Commentaries
HTR	*Harvard Theological Review*
HUT	Hermeneutische Untersuchungen zur Theologie
JBL	*Journal of Biblical Literature*
JSNT	*Journal for the Study of the New Testament*
JTS	*Journal of Theological Studies*
LEC	Library of Early Christianity
LW	*Luther's Works*. Edited by Jaroslav Pelikan and Helmut T. Lehmann. 55 vols. St. Louis: Concordia; Philadelphia: Fortress Press, 1958–1986.
NICNT	New International Commentary on the New Testament
NIGTC	New International Greek Testament Commentary

NovT	*Novum Testamentum*
NTS	*New Testament Studies*
OBT	Overtures to Biblical Theology
SBLDS	Society of Biblical Literature Dissertation Series
SemeiaSt	Semeia Studies
WUNT	Wissenschaftliche Untersuchungen zum Neuen Testament

Ancient Authors and Texts

Aristotle
- ***Nic. Eth.*** *Nicomachean Ethics*
- ***Rhet.*** *Rhetoric*

Cicero
- ***De or.*** *De oratore*

Clement of Alexandria
- ***Strom.*** *Stromata*

Dio Cassius
- ***Hist.*** *Roman History*

Dio Chrysostom
- ***Or.*** *Orations*
- ***Diog.*** *Diognetus*

Epictetus
- ***Diatr.*** *Diatribai (Dissertationes)*

Epiphanius
- ***Pan.*** *Panarion (Adversus Haereses)*

Irenaeus
- ***Adv. haer.*** *Adversus haereses*

John Chrysostom
- ***Hom. 1 Cor.*** *Homiliae in epistulam i ad Corinthios*
- ***Hom. Act.*** *Homiliae in Acta apostolorum*
- ***Hom. Heb.*** *Homiliae in epistulam ad Hebraeos*

Josephus
- ***J.W.*** *Jewish War*

Origen

C. Cels.	*Contra Celsum*
De princ.	*De principiis*

Philo

Cher.	*De cherubim*
Embassy	*On the Embassy to Gaius (= Legat.)*
Fug.	*De fuga et inventione*
Opif.	*De opificio mundi*
Post.	*De posteritate Caini*

Seneca

Ben.	*De beneficiis*

Strabo

Geog.	*Geographica*

Tatian

Ad gr.	*Oratio ad Graecos*

Tertullian

Prax.	*Adversus Praxean*
Virg.	*De virginibus velandis*

1 Corinthians

Laura Nasrallah

Introduction

First Corinthians is not the first letter that Paul and his coworkers wrote to those in Christ at Corinth (1 Cor. 5:9), but is part of a pattern of correspondence (7:1; 8:1; 12:1), oral reporting (1:11; 5:1), and visits from travelers (1:11; 4:7). This letter from Paul and Sosthenes to the community was penned from Ephesus (1 Cor. 16:8, 19) and dates to approximately 52 or 54 CE. The gift of the Corinthian correspondence, unique in the New Testament, is that it includes more than one authentic letter, allowing for historical reconstruction of a community's relationship with Paul over time. The letters collected in 2 Corinthians allow us to see that 1 Corinthians did not meet with universal success at Corinth. Second Corinthians 2:4, for example, mentions a letter of tears, and 2 Cor. 10:1–13:20 may be that letter of tears, in which Paul claims he has to act like a fool and boast. The passages 2 Cor. 2:14–6:13 and 7:2–4 together form an *apologia*, or defense, of Paul's apostleship. Because we have multiple letters to Corinth, we can glean more data and form a richer interpretation of productive struggle regarding ideas and practices over time between Paul and the Corinthians, between Paul and other traveling religious teachers, and, likely, among the Corinthians.

After nearly two millennia of study and commentaries on Paul's letters, the task of the commentator is more to curate what she or he thinks are important data and interpretations than to offer something new. But one contribution this commentary makes is that it joins other scholarly work that elucidates not what Paul meant in his communications with the Corinthians but the possible responses of the community in Christ. It considers what the participants in the *ekklēsia* had at hand in Roman Corinth theologically, religiously, politically, and socially.

That is, what were the conditions out of which those in Christ developed their rituals and beliefs, made ethical and political choices, and evaluated Paul's critiques and suggestions?

Ekklēsia

If we move the focus away from Paul—ignoring the binary of whether he was a heroic apostle or a traitor to Christ's true message (the latter was Thomas Jefferson's view), and turn instead to the communities to which he wrote (Johnson-DeBaufre and Nasrallah), we must ask what *ekklēsia*, their word for themselves, may have meant. What did it signal about how their community worked or how they ideally envisioned themselves? Some have argued that the term is a translation of the Hebrew *qahal*, a congregation. Certainly, Jewish associations, which used the Greek term *synagōgē*, existed in the Diaspora and attracted gentile converts and allies. Some have argued that *ekklēsia* signals the similarity of these earliest communities in Christ to so-called voluntary associations—guilds of people who gathered based on their employment (a guild of textile workers, for instance)—whose community together included worship of a god, meals, and often financial contributions (Ascough et al.). Some have pointed out similarities to philosophical schools (Stowers 2011b). Recent scholarship has shown that many associations were quite small (Kloppenborg). We should not assume that those to whom Paul wrote understood themselves to be, or to be in the process of becoming, a tight-knit, unified community (Stowers, 2011c). Further, the common translation for *ekklēsia*, "church," risks picturing something anachronistic.

Those who heard the term *ekklēsia* in antiquity may have understood a range of meanings, but certainly a political, civic assembly would have been evoked in an urban context (to which Paul's letters are aimed, after all: Meeks 2003). The term in the classical period had referred to the democratic assembly of the city, usually made up of free adult male citizens. At the time of Paul's writings, political assemblies in Greek cities around the Roman Empire still bore the name *ekklēsiai*, or in the singular, *ekklēsia*, and still met to engage in democratic deliberation about what was best for their cities (Miller). Were the *ekklēsiai* to which Paul wrote places of democratic debate and deliberative discourse, of authoritative speeches and challenges to those speeches, of the busy roil of argument, struggle, and the testing of ideas (Schüssler Fiorenza 1987; 1993)?

In this short commentary, I use the term *ekklēsia* instead of church. I also avoid using the term "Christian," since applying it to Paul's letters would be anachronistic: the term was coined only approximately forty years after the writing of 1 Corinthians (see Pliny, *Ep.*10.96; the statement in Acts 11:26 represents Luke's significantly later view). Moreover, while Paul had experienced an important change in identity, it was not to a known quantity called Christianity. Paul described himself as a Jew (e.g., Gal. 2:15)—a good Jew (Stendahl; Gager; Eisenbaum)—who had had a revelation of Christ and who was now called to communicate to "the nations" (NRSV: "Gentiles") about the righteousness of God that was available through faith (*pistis*) in this Christ (*christos*, the Greek translation of the Hebrew word that we render "Messiah" in English).

The Sociopolitical Context of Roman Corinth

To better understand the religious, political, and socioeconomic context within which the Corinthian *ekklēsia* developed their new identity in Christ, we must investigate Roman Corinth. In 146 BCE, the forces of the Roman general Mummius destroyed the city. It survived in a diminished form until Julius Caesar reestablished it as a Roman colony in 44 BCE, after which time it again emerged as a leader on the Peloponnesus. Corinth lay on a significant trade route in antiquity, on the isthmus connecting ancient Attica to the Peloponnesus. It nestled inland between its ports of Lechaion to the north and Kenchreai to the south, and near Isthmia, a town renowned for its quadrennial games. To transfer cargo from the Saronic Gulf to the southeast to the Gulf of Corinth to the northwest, ships had to negotiate with Corinth, unless they wanted to circumnavigate the Peloponnesus (Strabo, *Geog.* 8.6.20). Julius Caesar, Nero, and Herodes Atticus all attempted to dig a canal across the isthmus near Corinth, but failed, leaving it to Corinth to control a seven-meter-wide paved roadway (*diolkos*) that allowed oxen to drag ships or cargo across the narrow spit of land. Analysis of ceramic finds indicates Corinth's importance in trade (Slane).

Who made up the new, Roman Corinth? In literature of the first century BCE, the city is characterized by its tragic history and as a site of grief (Cicero, *Tusc.*3.53; Nasrallah 2012). Some inhabitants remained in the region between 146 BCE and the city's refounding as a Roman colony in 44 BCE, but Corinth was largely resettled at that time. Unlike many Roman colonies, Corinth was repopulated not by military veterans but by ex-slaves. Numismatic evidence indicates that a mix of freedpersons—former slaves—and traders became leaders in Corinth upon the founding of the new colony (Spawforth). Although freedpersons were not usually eligible for magistracies, Caesar made exceptions for colonies he founded (Millis 2010; 2013; Williams). Thus some characterized the city as populated by "a mass of good-for-nothing slaves," in first-century-BCE poet Crinagoras's language (Harrill, 71; Spawforth, 169). Yet the rhetoric about low-status freedpersons may be precisely aimed to discredit the high-status freedpersons who emigrated to Corinth to take advantage of this commercial hub (Millis 2013).

Thus it may not be coincidental that in a letter to Corinth we find the only use in the New Testament of the technical term "freedperson" (*apeleutheros*, 7:22). Some freedmen in Corinth held high civic positions and the Forum was marked by the benefactions of ex-slaves. Paul's words "Let . . . those . . . who buy [be] as though they had no possessions, and those who deal with the world as though they had no dealings with it" (7:29–31) would have been particularly thought-provoking to Corinthians-in-Christ in an urban setting in which buying and dealings with the world were central to civic identity—and in which having been bought and later manumitted were part of the identity of local elites (Nasrallah 2013).

Ethnicity and Identity in Roman Corinth
The City and the Ekklēsia

Given this history, what about ethnicity in Roman Corinth? Paul writes as a Jew who both asserts and reframes his ethnicity (9:19–22) to a community that is largely gentile (e.g., 12:2). We should not be surprised that gentiles sometimes wished to affiliate with Jews and even to shift their ethnicity and to become Jewish (Lieu; Cohen). Although archaeological evidence of Jews at Corinth is late and meager (a poorly incised lintel that once read "Synagogue of the Hebrews"; an impost capital with three menorahs), Philo mentions Corinth as having a Jewish population (*Legat.* 281) and Josephus states that Vespasian sent six thousand Jews to Corinth to work as slaves in the canal across the isthmus that Nero was attempting (*J.W.* 3.540; Millis 2010).

Although those to whom Paul wrote at Corinth were mostly gentiles, their choice to affiliate with Jews in Christ meant a shift in their ethnicity. In 1 Cor. 10:1, Paul argues that "our fathers were all under the cloud," referring to the story of Moses leading them through the Red Sea, and thus writing gentiles into the story of Israel. Such shifts in, debates about, and reflections on ethnicity were not rare in Roman Corinth (Concannon); the historical and mythical prestige of the city's Greek past was highlighted, even in the Roman period, through monuments and through the dissemination of iconography associated with the myths of Corinth (Robinson). Yet the city's dominant Romanness is signaled by a vast majority of its public inscriptions that appear in Latin only (Millis 2010).

In 2 Corinthians, Paul fights opponents whom he mockingly calls "super-apostles," but in 1 Corinthians he struggles with the Corinthian community itself, or at least with some members of it. The cause of this struggle has been the subject of debate. A variety of theories have been presented regarding the theological-philosophical inclinations of these Corinthians in Christ and their interest in being "spiritual people." The thesis of F. C. Baur (1831) and others, of Judaizers or other Christian factions as outside opponents, has largely been left behind. In the mid-twentieth century, Walter Schmithals's theory that the Corinthian community tended toward "a pneumatic-libertine Gnosticism," which was at the same time Jewish, was popular. Hans Conzelmann qualified this by calling the Corinthians "proto-Gnostic," employed the label "Corinthian libertinism," and talked about their "enthusiastic individualism." More recent scholarship demonstrates that we cannot discover a pre-Christian "Gnosticism" that may have affected the Corinthians, as Schmithals maintained (Pétrement 1990; K. King).

Scholars have long characterized the Corinthians as gnostics, libertines, Judaizers, and especially individualists, concerned about their private spiritual success rather than that of the community. Such approaches assume that Paul's letter neutrally records events and that his viewpoint is normative (see Wire; Castelli; Schüssler Fiorenza 1999). Instead, 1 Corinthians should be investigated as part of a larger correspondence, some of which is lost to us, that provides data about a community that included men and women, poor persons and those at or above subsistence level, slaves and freedpersons and free, who sometimes accepted and sometimes resisted Paul's characterizations of them. The Corinthian correspondence indicates a context of deliberative debate as happened so often in the civic *ekklēsia*—of back and forth, of struggling together toward a better future. Paul's letters are written to particular communities about particular situations; they are not systematic theology or doctrine in their first instantiation. He uses his rhetorical arts to persuade the Corinthians, and we can use the letter to reconstruct vibrant debates at the very beginnings of what we have come to call Christianity.

Those debates were conducted as the appointed time was "growing short" (7:29–31; 15:51–57). Paul and the communities to which he wrote, like many who framed their lives in terms of Jewish apocalyptic thought, understood themselves to be awaiting the imminent end of the age and the *parousia* ("appearance") of Christ. Nonetheless, their attention is focused in this letter on things great and small: the resurrection of the body, what they should eat, whether they should have sex, to give a few examples.

Paul has been characterized as promoting faith over law and works. Readers often approach 1 Corinthians in light of Paul's emphasis on faith and as a letter enjoining early Christian morality. Indeed, much of 1 Corinthians *is* about making ethical and practical choices in the world, and faith—faith in Christ, God's faithfulness, a concept that Paul explains in light of God's covenant with Abram (Gen 12:3; see Gal 3:6–18) and in the midst of a Jewish discussion about how God's faithfulness may or may not extend to "the nations," or gentiles—is central to Paul's letters. But when we look more closely, we realize that the binary of faith versus works may need dissolution and that the vague language of morality may not be adequate. Paul's writings about "morality" involve *practices* of communities in Christ, something we could even call "works." Is faith itself a matter of practice, or works? First Corinthians is, after all, very much about sex and eating, and even about whether Paul is owed a wage, as much as it is about things we might label more spiritual or faith-based: wisdom, spiritual gifts, and the resurrection.

The Text

The complex work of reconstructing the Corinthians in Christ is made somewhat easier because, other than some arguments about the place of 1 Corinthians 15 in the letter, most scholars agree that 1 Corinthians is a unified letter. In addition, it has few text-critical issues: its Greek text is remarkably uniform in various manuscripts (Fitzmyer, 63). It employs deliberative rhetoric (Conzelmann; Schüssler Fiorenza 1987; Mitchell 1991), the "political address of recommendation and dissuasion" that focuses on the future time as its subject of deliberation, urging audiences to pursue a course of action for the future, and often employs language of concord or harmony (Mitchell 1991).

Outline of the Letter

Chapters 1-4 of the letter contain the greeting and the *stasis*, or main point of the letter, and are characterized by a discussion of wisdom and an argument regarding how the Corinthians ought to think of themselves: they are not quite as spiritual as they thought themselves to be. In 5:1–11:1, Paul discusses particular case studies in ethical and theological practice, treating especially themes of sex and eating, as well as discussing the marital, ethnic, and social conditions in which persons may have been "called" to be in Christ. In 11:2–14:40, Paul treats further issues of practice in the *ekklēsia*, ranking the spiritual gifts the community experienced and seeking to control their use. Paul grounds these discussions in the political rhetoric of unity and "one body." In chapter 15, Paul turns to the topic of the resurrection of the dead, bringing together the cosmological hints about wisdom and the cosmos in chapters 1-4, together with concerns about the body's purity and practices in 5–11:1 and interest in the spiritual in 11:2–14:40. The epistolary closing comes in chapter 16.

Conclusions

According to the style of this volume, each section of my commentary on 1 Corinthians will be divided into three subsections: "the text in its ancient context," "the text in the interpretive tradition," and "the text in contemporary discussion." These divisions are heuristic. We should not think we have access to an ancient context that is pure data, neither disturbed nor enriched by our contemporary situations and by the long interpretative tradition. There is no true division between what the text meant and what it means today. Rather, we can use our locations of interpretation to open new questions about these ancient texts, and we can turn a critical eye to the limitations of our own locations. That is, we should approach the text with a *disciplined intimacy*, acknowledging the feeling of closeness that we may have with this text, whether as Christians, or because the text communicates important and recognizable ethical or political injunctions, or on account of the sheer pleasure of discovering something about ancient history. But we should also pursue the discipline of distance, acknowledging that the text was written in a time, language, and context not our own and that its values and injunctions, as well as the conditions of the social, political, and economic world in which it was produced, may surprise us.

1 Corinthians 1:1–17

Letter Writing and Community

The Text in Its Ancient Context

As is typical of ancient letters, 1 Corinthians begins with the *superscriptio*: "Paul, called to be an apostle of Christ Jesus by the will of God" (1:1). In other letters, Paul begins by introducing himself as "Paul, slave [*doulos*, sometimes translated more weakly as "servant"] of Jesus Christ" (Rom. 1:1, a letter in which he likely recommends himself to a community he doesn't know; see also Phil. 1:1) or "Paul, prisoner" (Philem. 1:1). The comparatively forceful *superscriptio* here introduces two key issues that follow in the letter. The first is the term *klētos*, "called" or "chosen." The letter uses this term and its cognates to talk about Paul's and the Corinthians' status. The addressees are described as "*chosen* holy ones" (1:2); "you were *called* into the fellowship of his [God's] son" (1:9). The issue of "calling" arises again in chapter 7. The second is the term *apostolos*, "one who is sent." As the letter ends, in 1 Cor. 15:9, Paul calls himself "least of the apostles," "unfit *to becalled* an apostle," yet elsewhere in the letter he asserts his role as laying a foundation (3:10) and as a father (4:14–21), as well as his ability to shape-shift depending on audience (9:19–22).

If we look more closely at the *superscriptio* of this letter and others, we see that the majority are cowritten: Silvanus and Timothy are cowriters of 1 Thessalonians; Timothy again is cowriter of the Letter to the Philippians. Romans 16:22 reveals an amanuensis: "I, Tertius, the writer of this letter, greet you in the Lord." In addition, some delivered letters and traveled on behalf of Paul and various *ekklēsiai*, such as Timothy and Epaphroditus. First Corinthians is cowritten by Sosthenes, "brother." These are not just the letters of Paul; they invoke and evoke an entire network of writers, deliverers, and readers. The writing desk becomes crowded with coworkers and perhaps slaves and freedmen, former slaves, since people of such status were often responsible for penning and delivering letters (Mouritsen).

The extended sentence, which is also a statement of thanksgiving (1:4–8), reveals four key issues of the letter. *Charis* (v. 4), often translated "grace," also means "favor" or "delight." A form of this word appears again at verse 7, *charisma*, often translated "spiritual gift": the idea of gifts of God or God's grace, and the question of how these "gifts" should be used and ranked, become key issues in chapters 11-14. Second, the word *eploutisthēte*, "you were enriched," appears in verse 5; the letter will later challenge the Corinthians precisely on issues of spiritual and material wealth and poverty. Paul will characterize the Corinthians as "what is low and despised in this world" (1:28). Mention of hunger and of some who "have not" indicates that some within the Corinthian community are poor (11:22). Third, the phrase "in speech [*logos*] and knowledge [*gnōsis*] of every kind" (1:5) signals debates about lofty or lowly speech and about what truly constitutes knowledge (1 Corinthians 1-4; 13:2, 9, 12). Fourth, verse 8 signals the letter's concern with the end time (the "day of the Lord"), a theme that arises especially at 1 Cor. 7:29–31 ("time growing short") and in the discussion in 1 Corinthians 15 of material transformation and the last trumpet. Grace and gifts, poverty and wealth literal and metaphorical, word or speech and knowledge, and the coming day of the Lord: these four themes, introduced early in the letter in the traditional epistolary location for a prayer or thanksgiving, will weave their way throughout this letter.

The *stasis*, or main point of the letter, emerges at 1 Cor. 1:10: "Now I appeal to you, brothers and sisters, by the name of our Lord Jesus Christ, that all of you be in agreement and that there be no divisions among you, but that you be united [or "reconciled"] in the same mind and the same purpose." Some take this thesis statement as Paul's description of a historical fact and have attempted to outline various "factions" of the community, following on Paul's characterization of the community as stating "I belong to Apollos" or "I belong to Paul," based on whomever had baptized them. But we do not know if all the Corinthians would have accepted Paul's assessment, and indeed, it seems that Paul has to argue rather hard for his role as the one who "planted" the community (1 Cor. 3:4–23). His arguments may have met with little success, given his admission that others have successfully influenced the community at Corinth (2 Corinthians). Paul turns from this interest in baptism (which will appear elsewhere in the letter) to emphasize "the cross of Christ" and Paul's own preaching, which happens "not in persuasive words of wisdom but in a demonstration of spirit and power" (2:4).

The Text in the Interpretive Tradition

John Chrysostom, a church leader from Antioch, was made archbishop of Constantinople in 397 CE. A well-known champion of Paul (Mitchell 2002), Chrysostom in some ways set forth what would become the mainstream Protestant understanding of a humble, suffering Paul among other apostles. Chrysostom focused on 1 Cor. 1:12 ("I belong to Paul . . .") and emphasized that Paul placed Peter last in this sequence to give Peter greater honor, despising any glory for himself. Chrysostom celebrated Paul's lack of eloquence in good homiletic fashion, with an anecdote: he once heard a "Greek" and a Christian arguing about whether Plato or Paul was superior. The Christian was wrong, Chrysostom argued, in trying "to establish that Paul was more learned than Plato." "For if Paul was uneducated and defeated Plato, the victory (as I have said) was glorious. . . . from this is it clear that his preaching has prevailed not by human wisdom but by the grace of God" (*Hom.* 3; Kovacs, 20–21). Chrysostom emphasizes the uneducated and common nature of early Christians, using Paul as a focal point to develop a well-known Christian trope, geographically widespread, that Christian identity was rooted in humble fishermen yet now elevated even women, fishermen, and the ignorant to a philosophical life (the Syrian Tatian, *Ad gr.*32.1–3; the Carthaginian Tertullian, *De an.* 3; the Alexandrian Origen, *C. Cels.* 3.44, 50). Paul's rhetoric in 1 Corinthians concerning his own ineloquence and his inversion of wisdom and folly fit well with early Christian self-definition as simple and humble, yet triumphing over the sophistication of the world, even though the early Christian men who used this trope were themselves quite sophisticated, educated, and powerful. Many Christians today, too, stand in an ambivalent relationship to certain forms of education and knowledge; it may be helpful to recognize that sometimes it is those who are well-educated who use the powerful persuasive trope of Christian simplicity and revelation.

The Text in Contemporary Discussion

The Second Vatican Council's "Decree on Ecumenism, *Unitatis redintegratio*" alludes to 1 Cor. 1:13 at its beginning.

> The restoration of unity among all Christians is one of the principal concerns of the Second Vatican Council. Christ the Lord founded one Church and one Church only. However, many Christian communions present themselves to men as the true inheritors of Jesus Christ; all indeed profess to be followers of the Lord but differ in mind and go their different ways, *as if Christ Himself were divided*. ("Decree on Ecumenism, *Unitatis redintegratio* 1)

More recently, the World Council of Churches has declared as the theme for the "Week of Prayer for Christian Unity" the question, "Has Christ been divided?" (1 Cor. 1:1–17).

Paul's evaluation that the Corinthians were divided and his injunction that they must be unified in one body was powerful in the past and is powerful today. This letter's language of unity draws from common political tropes of its time. *Homonoia* in Greek and *concordia* in Latin were terms used by various cities of the Greek East, for example on their coins, to assert a harmony that was the hard-won result of civic power plays. Paul's rhetoric of "one body" takes part in a broader discourse of unity that we know from the political rhetoric of the early Roman Empire (Mitchell 1991). Yet, today, in reading this rhetoric of unity in 1 Corinthians both scholarly and Christian communities often take for granted that Paul's characterization of Corinthian schism was an accurate description of problems at Corinth and do not inquire whether the Corinthians might have disagreed. Rhetoric of schism and unity is powerful whether in antiquity or today; it can be used to affirm community, but it also can be used to exclude or shame those who disagree.

1 Corinthians 1:18–4:21

Spirit and Wisdom

The Text in Its Ancient Context

The first four chapters of the letter move contrapuntally among the themes of Paul's role, the Corinthians' identity, spirit, and wisdom. The theme of wisdom was likely part of a long-standing conversation that was ongoing among the Corinthians in Christ; in this letter we find the term "wisdom" (*sophia*) seventeen times in contrast to its scant appearance elsewhere in Paul's genuine epistles (once in Romans and once in 2 Corinthians); so, too, *sophos* ("wise") appears eleven times in 1 Corinthians and four times in Romans, among the Pauline Epistles. Paul's letters reflect and discuss topics important to those to whom he wrote: obviously wisdom was a major theme among those at Corinth (Koester, 55–62). Paul takes an instructive tone in these chapters, one that might lead us to think that the Corinthians did not know much about wisdom or knowledge. Yet chapters 11-14 indicate that the Corinthians engaged in community practices that embodied and demonstrated their links to spirit and wisdom through "spiritual gifts." (I here leave the term "spirit" uncapitalized so that we do not read it through the lens of later Trinitarian ideas.)

Paul uses the rhetorical technique of developing his *ēthos*; that is, as Aristotle discusses it (*Rhet.* 1.2.1356a.4–12), the speaker describes himself in such a way as to make the audience sympathetic to him. Paul says that he did not come offering a testimony with lofty words or wisdom (2:1); he elaborates the common trope in which an orator talks about the simplicity and lack of education of his words over and against others—a simplicity and lack of education that then lends authenticity, truth, and power to his writing or speech. But Paul also may be making lemonade out of a lemon, since his opponents, it seems, characterize his person and speech in person as "weak" and "nothing" (2 Cor. 10:10). Paul places as central "Jesus Christ, and him crucified" (2:2), a "stumbling block" and weakness and scandal; Paul's juxtaposition of his own weakness with Christ's paradoxically elevates Paul: he is like Christ. In addition, with this language he may align himself with some in the community who are being called "weak," who are less educated and have concerns about being invaded by external, polluting forces.

First Corinthians 1:18–4:21 focuses on wisdom, yet questions what it (or she—the word is feminine in Greek: see below) truly is. Paul has just mentioned his role not as baptizer but as someone who preaches the gospel "not with wisdom," "lest the cross of Christ be emptied." Here the historical datum of the cross—a shameful criminal execution that predates the writing of this letter by only twenty years or so—is laid on a cosmological scale. It is understood to represent "the power of God" (1:18). Paul asserts—or perhaps admits—that the "word" (the term *logos* in Greek can mean "word," "speech," or "reason") of the cross is folly. The letter troubles the common sense that wisdom is good while folly is bad. The wisdom and folly of this world or universe (*tou kosmou*, 1:20, 28; also *kata sarka*,"according to flesh," 1:26; and *tou aiōnos toutou*, "of this age," 1:20, referring to the "debater") are contrasted to the wisdom and folly of God. The two are inversely related: God has made foolish the wisdom of this world (1:20); "what we preach" is in fact folly (*mōria*, 1:21).

Because of the emphasis on wisdom and knowledge (*gnōsis*), as well as the labels *sarkikoi or sarkinoi*, *psychikoi*, and *pneumatikoi*—that is, Paul's labeling certain people according to the terms "flesh," "soul," and "spirit"—in these early chapters of 1 Corinthians, twentieth-century scholars hypothesized either that the Corinthians were "gnostics" or that they were influenced by "gnostic" missionaries (Schmithals). But the language of wisdom and knowledge is not only found in materials we might label "gnostic"—for example, the texts found at Nag

Hammadi and the points of view polemically treated by writers like Irenaeus and others—but also in Jewish texts that speculate about the creation of humans (esp. Gen. 2:7), divine inbreathing at creation, and the human potential for knowledge, wisdom, and being like God. Moreover, "Gnosticism" was not an established or unified school in the first century. The term itself is a later invention emerging from early Christian polemics, then reified in modern scholarship (K. King).

The language of wisdom at Corinth emerges in a context of many traditions that honored wisdom and knowledge in the ancient world, whether Jews, members of philosophical schools, or those who honored a goddess like Isis; it emerged in the context of rich philosophical debates and diverse stories about the creation of the world, including much debate over the interpretation of Plato's *Timaeus*. Paul and the Corinthians perhaps had different understandings of the terminology of wisdom and knowledge, of flesh, soul, and spirit. But in their deployment of such language they stood in a conversation that preceded and would follow them about how creation happened and whether and how humans might know the divine in the present, as Jews and Christians alike debated the meaning and significance of a creation out of the clay or earth in Genesis 2 and reference to creation of the human in God's image in Genesis 1. Such Jewish and Christian debates about wisdom and knowledge, about flesh, soul, and spirit, happened in the context of a culture that produced images of the gods in human form, and happened in conversation with Greek philosophical texts and with the strong traditions of wisdom theology in Judaism, characterized by texts like Ben Sira and the Wisdom of Solomon, among many others.

Scholars have long situated 1 Corinthians within Hellenistic Jewish discourses on wisdom (e.g., Wilckens; Horsley; Sterling). There must have been at Corinth deep and rich debates about the nature of God and creation, about how God works and is manifest in the world, which drew from the wisdom theologies of Judaism. Proverbs 8:22 offers a famously clear statement of Wisdom personified as cocreator of the world with God (the Greek word *sophia* is grammatically feminine; see also Philo, *Cher.* 49 on God as "the husband of Sophia"). Other traditions, exemplified in the early-first-century CE Jewish writer Philo of Alexandria, seem to understand Sophia and Logos as related or interchangeable figures who are divine characters themselves; Philo talks about the Logos of God as the instrument by which God made creation (*Cher.* 127); elsewhere, the Logos is the image of God, in closest proximity to God, and the "charioteer" above all the other divine powers (*Fug.* 100; see also Philo, *Post.* 78; *Fug.* 97; Horsley 1979; Grabbe; Boyarin 2001).

Some (or many) within the Corinthian *ekklēsia* likely considered Sophia—Wisdom personified—to be a power of God that was significant for their theology and for their understanding of themselves. Jesus as Sophia or as a prophet of Sophia is well attested in earliest Gospel traditions (e.g., Luke 7:34–36; Lamp; Schüssler Fiorenza 1994; Johnson-DeBaufre). In 1 Cor. 2:9, we find a quotation that alludes to the Jewish Scriptures and bears a striking resemblance to *Gospel of Thomas* 17 (see also Q/Lk 10:23–24; Koester, 58–59; Conzelmann, 63–64). Thus the Corinthians and Paul may have shared a source of Jesus sayings that involved wisdom, and perhaps they knew of theological traditions that employed terminology of hiddenness and revelation (see also 1 Cor. 2:7, 10; 3:13; 4:5; Koester, 55–56).

Indeed, the Corinthians may have understood Christ as Wisdom. Paul emphasizes Christ terminology instead and debates the meaning of *sophia*. For Paul, wisdom is not a divine power to be reckoned with, or a power that helps to perfect humans and render them friends of God, as she is depicted in the Wisdom of Solomon (from Alexandria, perhaps first century CE). Wisdom as cocreator of the world leaves only a faint trace in 1 Corinthians.

At Corinth, Wisdom is understood not only in terms of cosmology and theology but also in terms of sociology. The question of who has true wisdom and knowledge percolates throughout the letter. Paul extends a challenge: "Where is the one who is wise?" (1:20). In 1 Cor. 2:6, Paul renders wisdom into something he and others can impart, and only to the "perfect" or "initiates" (*teleioi*).

Paul discusses wisdom in ethnic terms in 1:22: *Ioudaioi* (which we can translate "Jews" or "Judeans"; see Cohen; Hodge) "ask for signs and

Greeks seek wisdom." How might Paul's characterization of ethnicity have gone over in Roman Corinth, with its famed Greek heritage, its new Roman status? In this passage, Paul proposes an alternative mixed ethnicity for the *ekklēsia* in Christ at Corinth, aligning them with "those who are the called[*klētoi*], both Jews and Greeks" (1:24). Paul defines the identity of the *ekklēsia* at Corinth as a chosenness that brings Jews and Greeks together.

The community may have understood itself as wise, as "called," and also as *teleioi*, which can be translated "perfect" or "complete" and is also the term for "initiates." "Yet among the *teleioi* we do speak wisdom . . . God's wisdom, secret and hidden, which God decreed before the ages," Paul declares (2:6–7). A Corinthian hearing this might reasonably think that she or he is one of the "perfect" who has received the spirit from God, rather than the "spirit of this cosmos" or world (2:12). Later in the letter it becomes clear that Corinthians engaged in practices of *pneumatika*, spiritual things or spiritual gifts (1 Corinthians 12-14). But Paul introduces another label: the *psychikos*, the "soul" person, who doesn't discern things as the *pneumatikos*, or "spirit person," does (2:14–15). Certainly any reader or hearer of the passage would prefer to fall into the "perfect" and "spiritual" category. The news gets worse: Paul states that he had to address them as *sarkinoi*, "flesh people" (3:1), feeding them only milk. Not only was this true in the past, but also "you are still of the flesh" (3:3) because of "strife" and claims like "I am of Paul, I am of Apollos."

Paul's accusation of dissension because of Corinthian attachment to one apostle or another reprises the thesis of the letter and allows him to segue again to the issue of apostleship and leadership that he had raised earlier (1 Cor. 1:10–16). In 3:5–4:21, he continues to raise questions about the roles he and Apollos played in the community; he depicts himself and Apollos in the language of household managers (3:5: *diakonoi*; 4:1: *hypēretas* and *oikonomous*). These roles are often taken by high-status slaves or freedpersons who have risen in the ranks of a household, promoted by their masters to more authoritative roles (Martin 1990). The Corinthians are depicted as passive, as a field to be planted or as something to be built (Wire).

Paul goes on to depict active, suffering apostles in contradistinction to the Corinthians. The apostles are "as though sentenced to death, because we have become a spectacle to the world, to angels and to mortals" (4:9). The language of death sentence and spectacle reminds us of the very real Roman practice of putting people to death and of spectacle (Frilingos), yet Paul's image does not limit itself to the Roman imperial context; the image he gives is of cosmic battle (so also at 2:8, "rulers of this age"). He contrasts the apostles' role as "refuse of the cosmos" (4:13) to the Corinthians, who are enriched and have come to reign (4:8). The apostles are "fools for the sake of Christ, but you are wise in Christ" (4:10).

Given the language of reversal that has already occurred regarding true wisdom and God's foolishness, the Corinthians would do well to be suspicious of this seeming praise. Indeed, Paul makes it explicit that he speaks to them as "beloved children" in need of admonition and he suggests to them that he is their sole father in the midst of many guides (4:15), a father who might come "with a stick" rather than "with love" (4:21). From chapter 1 to the end of chapter 4, leadership and authority in the Corinthian community has been reduced from four examples of possible mystagogues or leaders ("I am of Cephas," "I am of Apollos," "I am of Paul," "I am of Christ") to two (Paul and Apollos), to one, in his framing of himself as the singular father.

The Text in the Interpretive Tradition

Later Christians often used and debated the meaning of the discussion in 1 Corinthians 1-4 of wisdom and knowledge, as well as the question of which humans could be "spiritual," which "psychic" (from the term *psychē*, "soul," not to be confused with our modern meaning of the term!), and which "fleshly" (or, later, "hylic" or "material"). In the decades and centuries after Paul wrote, Christians wished to be *gnostikoi*, which we could woodenly translate "gnostics," but given the historical misuse of that term, perhaps "in the know" is a better translation. They wished to be *pneumatikoi*, spiritual people. These were values common to the ancient world and indeed today.

In the late second century CE, Irenaeus, a Christian writer in Gaul, would accuse some Christians, whom he said were "followers of Valentinus" (a Christian philosopher-theologian who likely lived a few decades prior) of a kind of determinism that assigned people to a certain fixed category, that would gut any motivations for ethical behavior, and that would limit salvation (*Adv. haer.* 1.6.2). In a Christian text such as the *Tripartite Tractate*, found among the so-called gnostic materials at Nag Hammadi, we find the statement:

> Now, humanity came to be according to three essential types—spiritual, physical, and material—reproducing the pattern of the three kinds of dispositions of the Logos, from which sprung material, physical, and spiritual beings. The essences of the three kinds can each be known by its fruit. (*Tripartite Tractate* 118.14–29, in Kocar 2013)

While Irenaeus would accuse such Christians of a determinism that condemned some humans to a permanent state of ignorance of the Father and no possibility of salvation, closer investigation of the *Tripartite Tractate* or indeed Irenaeus himself shows that Paul's writings in 1 Corinthians 1-4 instead inspired a great deal of later theological controversy over what constituted correct Christian practice and thinking, and how one could attain to the status of being spiritual or "in the know," truly *gnostikos*.

We find further evidence of how 1 Corinthians inspired later debates about wisdom in Origen, for example, who in the late second century or early third century explained that what is meant by the "wisdom of the rulers of this world" are the secret and hidden philosophies, astrologies, and magi of various nations, which may lead to demonic invasion. Christians, in contrast, are purified by abstinence and pure practices and receive prophecy and gifts in this way (*De princ.* 3.3). In the early sixth century, someone who took up the name of Dionysius the Areopagite (according to Acts, a convert at Athens after he heard Paul's speech there) and used Paul's language of Greeks seeking wisdom to rehabilitate the truth of Greek philosophy for Christian purposes

(Stang, 148–50). A variety of Christians found in 1 Corinthians' language of wisdom and knowledge a foundation from which to debate who could access such wisdom and knowledge and how.

The Text in Contemporary Discussion

The November 1993 conference "Re-Imagining: A Global Theological Conference by Women: for Men and Women" was an ecumenical meeting largely organized by U.S. Protestant denominations as part of the World Council of Churches' larger "Ecumenical Decade: Churches in Solidarity with Women," begun in 1988. The repeated chant "Bless Sophia" at this conference, among other things, led to accusations of goddess worship. Organizers are said to have grounded their emphasis on Sophia through recourse to Scriptures in Proverbs, Luke, and 1 Corinthians. Accusations that Sophia rather than Jesus was set forth as a "divine revealer" and concerns that Sophia was elevated to a divine level indicate that some ancient communities in Christ were more flexible and expansive in their Christology and theology than modern communities. We can think, for example, of language of Jesus as "the Sophia of God" in 1 Cor. 1:24 or of the flexibility of ancient Jewish and Christian traditions that describe a Sophia who existed at the beginning of the world with God and created the world with God. An emphasis on Wisdom or Sophia can be controversial in any age, even if canonical texts present Sophia as cocreator with God or as attribute of God, as a figure who sends out prophets like Jesus, and as a divine figure instantiated by Jesus. A theology—thealogy, we could say, emphasizing the possibilities of thinking of a God who transcends gender and/or is sometimes thought of in feminine terms—that takes into account the traditions of Sophia can support two kinds of work. First, it can undergird the work of those theologians, whether ancient or contemporary, who point out that attempts to name God definitively as Father or Mother or to fix our idea of God too firmly are idolatrous. Second, taking into account ancient traditions of Sophia in Judaism and Christianity can aid those who argue for women's leadership in Christian communities.

1 Corinthians 5:1–6:11

Insiders, Outsiders, and Judgment

The Text in Its Ancient Context

Paul has introduced the idea that the Corinthians are not at the highest state of completion or initiation (*teleioi*) as spiritual people (*pneumatikoi*) and that he as father can correct them with love or with a stick (1 Cor. 4:21). In the pages that follow, Paul expands on the bad news that the Corinthians are not, in his opinion, at the level of spiritual or wise or perfected people. Paul treats particular examples of Corinthian practices that he seeks to correct.

He speaks against *porneia*, a broad term in the ancient world that the NRSV translates "immorality," but that among Jewish and Christian writings has tinges of sexual sin and of idolatry, which is often also sexualized as an improper relationship of a nation with a false god (see, e.g., Hosea 4:11; Revelation 17; Rom. 1:22–32). The theme of *porneia* echoes throughout the passage and reaches its apex in two vice lists at 5:9–11 and 6:9–10, lists that represent cultural understandings of disorder in the world and are typical discourse at the time, whether among those we would label Jews or those we would label Greco-Roman writers. On the one hand, Paul insists that the Corinthians were previously *pornoi* (NRSV: "fornicators") and idolaters (6:9); on the other hand, he describes them as "washed, made holy, made just [or righteous] in the name of the Lord Jesus Christ and in the spirit of our God" (6:11). This new state is called into question by the presence of some who are still *pornoi* among them, and the dangers of idolatry loom large in the following chapters.

Paul's first example is a man who "has" (a sexual euphemism) his father's wife, presumably his stepmother. This discussion of *porneia* reveals something larger about how Paul frames the community's identity. First, he roots the *ekklēsia* at Corinth in a Jewish identity by stating derogatorily that they have *porneia* among them that is not even found among "the nations" (5:1). Framing the man's sin as a contagion that can permeate the community like leaven that "puffs up" a lump of dough, he introduces the idea of Christ as Paschal sacrifice, indicating that he and/or those at Corinth followed early traditions (as in the Gospel of John) of Jesus as having been crucified on Passover. Paul's metaphor also assumes that the community will understand basic Passover practices. Second, Paul introduces explicitly the theme of insiders and outsiders. A quotation from Deut. 17:7, "Drive out the wicked person from among you" (5:13), not only shows that Paul expects the community at Corinth to make sense of references to Scripture, but also makes the point that it's God's business to worry about "those outside" and the Corinthians' business to worry about those "among" or "inside," a theme that will arise again with the question of outsiders' response to speaking in tongues (14:24–25). In 5:3–5, Paul suggests that when those in Christ at Corinth assemble, Paul's spirit is present and the community should deliver the man to Satan so that the man's flesh will be destroyed, but his spirit saved "in the day of our Lord" (5:5). What sort of ritual is imagined is unclear (perhaps even a death penalty? Gaca, 140), but the theme of spirit clearly carries through from the first four chapters into the rest of the letter, in which spiritual gifts are discussed as well as the idea of spiritual bodies.

From the case of the man with his stepmother emerges a larger point about judgment. Paul emphasizes that the Corinthians should be concerned with what is happening inside the community and with adjudicating—"judging"—things there. From the relatively mundane case at hand emerges a larger cosmological vision: the holy ones (*hagioi*, a term Paul and Sosthenes had applied to the Corinthians in 1:2) will judge the cosmos and the angels (6:2–3).

The Text in the Interpretive Tradition

John Calvin's mid-sixteenth-century commentary on 1 and 2 Corinthians eruditely surveys early church fathers' interpretations of these epistles, as well as offering his opinion, which is marked by the rise of the Protestant Reformation, in which Calvin was a key figure.

The insider-outsider language of 1 Corinthians is transferred to his contemporaneous situation of Protestant-Catholic relations and shows the malleability of Paul's text for various situations. Calvin notes that the passage about leaven and the true Passover "will also be of service for setting aside the sacrilege of the Papal mass. For Paul does not teach that Christ is offered daily, but that the sacrifice being offered up once for all, it remains that the spiritual feast be celebrated during our whole life" (Calvin, 189–90). Reference to the exclusion of the one called brother inspired Calvin momentarily to soften his antipapist tone, declaring that "no one may think that we ought to employ equally severe measures against those who, while at this day dispersed under the tyranny of the Pope, pollute themselves with many corrupt rites" (194). Inspired by Paul's line about not taking food with the brother who has offended, Calvin rails against "the Roman antichrist" that prohibits "any one from helping one that has been excommunicated to food, or fuel, or drink or any of the supports of life" (195). The way in which Calvin applies this passage to his own time reminds us of the larger history of interpretation of Paul's letters. Scholars and "lay" alike tend to define early Christianity over and against Jews (who have been characterized as particularistic and law-obsessed) and Catholics (who have been depicted as like "pagans" in their concern with works and ritual), as J. Z. Smith discusses in his *Drudgery Divine*. If we forget that Paul was a Jew and that many of his letters are concerned with very practical things, we may stand in danger of producing interpretations that read as anti-Jewish and anti-Catholic.

The Text in Contemporary Discussion

Paul's use of strong language of insiders and outsiders has inspired scholars to discuss 1 Corinthians through the lens of anthropology and sociology, reminding us that contemporary interpreters of Paul's writings include those outside of confessional Christian circles who find the letters useful for comparison with other times and places.

Theissen (1982), for example, explains various theological and ritual stances at Corinth as linked to varieties of socioeconomic status there and suggests that scholars should be in the business of comparing early Christian literatures with other religious phenomena of the world. Taking up such a challenge, Jonathan Z. Smith (2004) and Richard DeMaris (1995) have used anthropological insights to understand 1 Corinthians in a *local* context. The former shows the way in which 1 Corinthians has influenced discussions of "commensalism" (namely, relations with other local religions) and Christian revivalism in the local context of Papua New Guinea. The latter elucidates Corinthian references to spirit in light of ancestor cults and familial practices, evidenced in the archaeological record at Corinth.

Many have found anthropologist Mary Douglas's expounding of how the individual body is controlled and regulated (or not) in relation to the social body (a group) helpful for an analysis of the various viewpoints that might stand behind 1 Corinthians (e.g., Neyrey). Might some members of the *ekklēsia* have perceived the body as dangerously permeable, and sought to control sex, eating, spirit-possession, and relations with outsiders, while some saw the body as less dangerously subject to pollution? Dale Martin (1995) addresses the important question of how these perceptions—theological and medical—of the individual body affected ideas of the communal body.

These comparisons and insights help us to sharpen our understanding that 1 Corinthians deserves close attention and comparison with other phenomena in the history of religions. Paul's letters are not written to "us," whatever our time and place, even if his injunctions about holiness and purity, as well as his exhortations to unity, might be used in church debates today, for example about sexuality or sex acts. There is no "commonsense" reading that respects the complexity of these letters. They require a contextualization in their own time, in light of religious practices and beliefs in the first century, before they can be appropriated today.

1 Corinthians 6:12–7:40

"All Things Are Permitted to Me" and "Stay as You Are"

The Text in Its Ancient Context

Having insisted that those in Christ at Corinth were once, and in the present some still are, *pornoi*, Paul continues to treat the theme of immorality by quoting and questioning "slogans" that may be the Corinthians' own or that he assumes they will understand. In 6:12, we find "all things are permitted to me," met by Paul's commentary "but not all things are beneficial"; in 6:13, we find "food is meant for the stomach and the stomach for food," met by Paul's commentary "God will destroy both." With both verses, we find common structure; a rhetorical analysis shows the assertion of an idea, and then its qualification, which leads scholars to think that the assertion is an idea that the Corinthians have set forth, while the qualification is Paul's own response to the idea or slogan (Wire).

Paul takes the theme of his previous chapter and argues that the body (*sōma*) is not meant for *porneia* but for "the Lord" (6:13). *Sōma* in Greek signals the body proper; it signals the body politic (Mitchell 1991); it is also a term sometimes used for "slave." Throughout 1 Corinthians, the political force of the term *sōma* is deployed, as well as the frequent political rhetoric that the body should be unified. In Paul's thought, the Corinthians' bodies become members of, and come to constitute, the body of Christ (6:15), and so should communally maintain the purity of their body. The Corinthian community is also twice asked to think of itself as collectively "on the market," as if a slave body purchased by God. First Corinthians 6:19b–20 reads, "You are not your own; you were bought with a price. So glorify God in your body"; it is echoed by 7:23, "you were bought with a price; do not become slaves of humans." Participants in the *ekklēsia* at Corinth lived in a city steeped in the history of former slavery, refounded as it was by freedpersons; 1 Corinthians 7 makes clear that slaves are part of the community as well. Thus the language of *sōma* resonated at multiple levels, calling to mind the individual body and its morality, the slave body, and the communal body politic.

Paul argues that those to whom he writes should together "shun immorality," including associating with a prostitute. The conversation is framed toward a male audience that might "join" themselves (6:16) to a female. Jennifer Glancy interrogates the passage, wondering whether a slave would necessarily be excluded from the Corinthian body of Christ, since slaves were not able to control their bodies but could be subjected to *porneia* by their masters; ancient texts talk about slaves "used" by their masters as part of the "normal" operations of slavery, or a slave might be forced into prostitution (Marchal).

Paul reinforces his point about not joining one's body with a prostitute by using the metaphor of body as *naos*, or temple to the Lord. What temple is evoked? The Corinthians might be familiar with the kind of thought that Philo, for instance, exhibits when he interprets Genesis 2, describing Adam's body as a "shrine or sacred sanctuary" carrying within it the *agalma*, or "image," of the divine (*Opif.* 137). Given concerns expressed for a collection to be taken to Jerusalem (1 Cor. 16:1–4; 2 Corinthians 8–9), the temple in Jerusalem might be evoked. Given their location, one of the many temples of Corinth might be come to mind (Weissenrieder), each with its own *temenos*, or boundary, within which space is sacralized and only certain activities are allowed.

What are the appropriate practices of the individual body and the "body politic"? First Corinthians 7 extends this question to the circumstances of marriage, enslavement, and circumcision. The main theme of the chapter is to "remain as you are," which is elaborated in 7:17: "Only, let everyone lead the life which the Lord has assigned to him or her, and in which God has called him or her" (see Harrill). Here Paul reprises the significant theme of "call," which resounds throughout the letter and which was part of the unique ethnic and practical identity of the community at Corinth—recall that they are no longer Jews or Greeks, but "the called" (1:24). But this status as "the called" leads to an odd stasis rather than transformation: they may be called, but, depending on their place in society in Roman Corinth, the Corinthians may have been variously surprised, disappointed, or reassured to be told to remain as they are. Scholars still hotly debate the meaning of this passage, however, because of difficulties in understanding the Greek; Scott Bartchy has argued instead, for example, that Paul emphasizes that one's call in Christ is more significant than any social status, but that 1 Corinthians 7 does not encourage members of the community to remain enslaved. If we keep our attention on the question of the interpretation of those who first received the letter, we may reasonably surmise that they too debated the meaning of this section.

Some Corinthians likely understood their identity as "called" by Christ and the transforming ritual of baptism to lead to a present state of resurrection (Wire) and/or to upend the distinctions of a kyriarchal society—a term coined by Elisabeth Schüssler Fiorenza to point to intersecting structural injustices rooted in the rule of masters (*kyrioi*) over slaves, males over females. They might have disagreed with Paul's urgent call to remain in the state in which they had been called.

While marriage is a primary concern in chapter 7, we see all three of the socioeconomic and ethnic binaries of what is likely a pre-Pauline baptismal formula discussed here (marriage [male and female]: 7:1–16, 25–40; ethnicity [Jew nor Greek] in terms of circumcision as its sign: 7:18–20; slavery and manumission [neither slave nor free]: 7:21–24). We know that baptism was important to the community at Corinth (1:13–17) and that they practiced baptism on behalf of the dead (15:29). We can assume that the Corinthians used a standard pre-Pauline baptismal formula, since in 1 Cor. 12:13 Paul partially cites what are likely ritual words that we also know from Gal. 3:27–28: "As many of you as were baptized into Christ have clothed yourselves with Christ. There is no longer Jew or Greek, there is no longer slave or free, there is no longer male and female; for all of you are one in Christ Jesus."

The Corinthians likely had suggested to Paul that "it is good that a man not touch a woman," since he precedes this with "now concerning what you wrote." The Corinthians' practice may be rooted in expectations of an imminent end to time, or to larger cultural and philosophical discussions of desire and its extirpation; the popular philosophical idea of *enkrateia*, or self-control, is evoked in 7:9 with the word "they should control themselves." Philo, a Jew from Alexandria who was a near contemporary of Paul's, interpreted the entire Tenth Commandment as an injunction, "do not desire," and understood the Mosaic dietary laws as ascetic precepts that led to self-control (Svebakken), teaching how to keep the self inured to the buffets of outside attractions, whether of food or sex or prestige. Such philosophical practices as abstaining from sex and marriage might fly in the face of Augustan marriage laws. Later sources characterize the *Lex Julia de maritandis ordinibus* and the *Lex Julia de adulteriis coercendis* of 18–17 BCE as encouraging people to marry, enacting penalties for adultery, imposing financial penalties on unmarried men and women, and seeking to limit marriages so that those of senatorial status would not mix with those of lower status—thus a senator or his children were barred from marrying freedpersons, those involved in certain kinds of theater, and prostitutes (e.g., Dio Cassius, *Hist.* 54.16.1). These harsh reforms, which were presented as part of a family values campaign (Suetonius, *Life of Augustus* 34), were revised in 9 CE in the Lex Papia Poppaea, which used a carrot rather than a stick, preferring political candidates who had more children, allowing freedpersons who had more children substantial freedom from the patron-client relations with their former masters, and relieving from political responsibilities those who had a great number of children.

The discussion of marriage also reminds us that many at Corinth would hear these words in light of their own "mixed marriages" (Hodge), having to negotiate with or to be subject to a spouse who had different ethics and religious practices from their own. Paul's arguments indicate that he and perhaps the Corinthians shared some notion of an extended or communicable health or salvation (Hodge, 16): the one who is made holy can somehow extend that holiness to his or her spouse and render their children "saints" or "holy ones" (Hodge, 14).

Although chapter 7 focuses on marriage, Paul briefly treats circumcision and slavery, the two other categories of the pre-Pauline baptismal formula. He quickly argues that one should seek neither circumcision nor to remove the marks of circumcision. While Jewish men were not the only men to practice circumcision in antiquity, and while Jewish women were not circumcised, circumcision became a kind of metonymy for Jews (Cohen). In Galatians, Paul insists that circumcision is nothing, even though men in antiquity who affiliated with Judaism may have wished to participate fully in the covenants of Judaism, including circumcision: Paul instead offers an extended argument in Galatians that covenantal participation is possible without circumcision, since God brought Abra(ha)m into covenant with him before Abra(ha)m was circumcised.

Paul then proceeds to talk about slaves. Verse 20 asserts the larger theme of the chapter (Harrill), that "everyone should remain in the state in which he [or she] was called." It continues: "Were you a slave when called? Never mind. But if you can gain your freedom, rather use [it] [*mallon chrēsai*]." The last phrase is the subject of much controversy. The object of the Greek verb is unclear. Should they "use" their freedom? Their slavery? If we attend to the immediate grammatical context, we will conclude that they should use their freedom—that is, to seek manumission by some means. If we look at the overall message of chapter 7, with its banging repetition of "remain," we will conclude that we should supply "slavery." The grammatical uncertainty is not due to our weak grasp of first-century Greek: roughly three centuries after the writing of 1 Corinthians, John Chrysostom's community debated whether to supply "freedom" or "slavery" (*Hom. 1 Cor.* 19.5). The Corinthians who received this letter were likely as baffled as we. We may wonder whether they sought clarification from the carrier of Paul and Sosthenes's letter, who was likely a freedperson or slave; such letter carriers were often expected not only to deliver their masters' correspondence but also to voice and to interpret its contents (Mouritsen).

Many attempt to neutralize the passage's revolutionary idea of seeking freedom, on the one hand, or its horrifying quietism of staying enslaved, on the other, by reading the passage as "merely" eschatological or theological (e.g., Conzelmann; Horsley 1998). It is a reasonable choice after Paul's own phrasing in 7:29: "the appointed time has grown short" and the following passage, in which people are encouraged to live "as if not," with the conclusion that "the form of this cosmos [or world] is passing away" (7:31b). Many commentators impute to Paul (and thus to "his" churches) a disinterest in material conditions on account of expectation of an imminent *parousia* or appearance of Christ, but apocalyptic notions could equally lead to concrete political action such as the kind of revolutionary fervor Josephus mentions when he talks about Jewish prophets who led groups that opposed the Romans and were quashed. Others would argue that we should read Paul in light of popular philosophical movements like Stoicism that enjoin that gender and social status and economic opportunity should not matter if one rightly cultivates within oneself a philosophical lack of caring for external events (e.g., Philo, *Every Good Man Is Free*); Epictetus describes the slave who longs to be free, only to be freed and realize that he is enslaved by the need to supply himself with such things as food and clothes (*Diatr.* 4.1.33).

Such an approach misses the opportunity to think about material and social realities of slavery at Corinth (Nasrallah 2013). The Corinthians did not necessarily share Paul's argument to "remain as you are," and they may have debated what he meant by the elusive *mallon chrēsai*, "rather use." Perhaps they wished Paul had offered a clearer statement of social change in the present. Perhaps some of the Corinthians were aware of contemporaneous practices at Delphi and Kalymna, in which a slave was "sold" for freedom to a god and thus manumitted (Deissmann). Perhaps they preferred to think that baptism and their calling "in Christ" transformed ethnicity, gender, and social religions in the present, rather than accepting a present stasis followed by future transformation. Perhaps they found the divine to be inbreaking in the present, as evidenced in spiritual gifts or *pneumatika*, and understood their individual bodies and communal body alike to be based in a new calling rather than an old.

The Text in the Interpretive Tradition

Over the centuries, Christians have debated the merits of celibacy and marriage in clerical and lay life. While Paul prefers that people not marry, his injunctions in 1 Corinthians 7 allow for marriage, and even suggest that desire be recognized and channeled in marriage—thus that marriage exists not only for procreation but also as a locus of sexual morality. In 1523, Martin Luther wrote a treatise on 1 Corinthians 7, addressing it "to the August and honorable Hans Loser of Pretzsch," as a wedding gift, with the hopes that he will "no longer postpone your marriage" (Luther, 3). A pity for the bride, then, that Luther's treatise proper starts with the words "What a fool is he who takes a wife, says the world, and it is certainly true" (5). Of course, Luther goes on, like Paul, to point out the folly of this worldly wisdom, as well as to use Paul as a tool against the Roman Catholicism of his day. Luther states that he has taken on the task of interpreting 1 Corinthians 7 because "this very chapter, more than all the other writings of the entire Bible, has been twisted back and forth to condemn the married state and at the same time to give a strong appearance of sanctity to the dangers and peculiar state of celibacy" (3).

So too, in the ancient world, Paul's teachings on marriage were used in two opposing directions. Two examples will suffice to show how 1 Corinthians 7 was interpreted in radically different ways soon after it was written. First Timothy, written in Paul's name at the end of the first century or beginning of the second, insists that those who have the task of "bishop" should be married, although only once (3:2), and that "she" (whether Eve or women more generally is unclear) "will be saved through bearing children" (1 Tim. 2:15). The *Acts of Paul and Thecla*, a text embodying traditions circulating in the second century CE, insists that Paul blessed celibacy, and focuses on the story of a young woman, Thecla, who follows Paul and renounces her betrothal for a life of celibacy.

The Text in Contemporary Discussion

The phrase "the appointed time has grown short" (7:29) has attracted recent attention by political philosophers and other scholars. Following on Walter Benjamin's *Theses on the Philosophy of History*, they expand on the idea of "messianic time" and find in Paul's writings a sense of crisis that has the potential to inspire new ways of thinking about being in the present. Giorgio Agamben is particularly interested in the use in 1 Cor. 7:29 of the term *synestalmenos* ("drawn together" or "shortened" like a sail) to discuss time (*kairos*) (Agamben, 62). Alain Badiou describes Paul as "poet-thinker of the event" and a "militant figure"; Paul is to Jesus as Lenin was to Marx (as Slavoj Žižek also argues). Even more than Jesus, Badiou argues, Paul marked a break in what he calls "evental time": that is, for Paul, the resurrection changed everything.

Paul's letters and the sort of apocalyptic thinking we find in 1 Corinthians 7 are worthy resources for political philosophy. But Badiou and others, in part because of their only cursory understanding of Paul's historical context, have misused and mischaracterized Paul as a hero of universalism. For example, while recognizing Paul as a Jew, Badiou has nonetheless supported anti-Jewish interpretation by emphasizing Paul as a universalist thinker above the particulars of Judaism (Badiou, 13, 23); despite his claimed interest in universality, Badiou sweeps Paul's statements about women under the carpet by seeing them as only "cultural" (103–4). Badiou and others have produced a Paul who is an "anti-philosophical theoretician of universality," who is uniquely right over and against the "opinions" of those to whom he writes; they have elaborated a Paul who in relation to messianic or "evental" time argues for a truth that is produced by the subject, without recognizing that the subject they celebrate looks awfully like a "rational," universal male (Dunning).

The transformative theological and political idea of the *eschaton* and "messianic time," which Agamben, Badiou, and others correctly see in Paul's letters, does not reach full potential in these contemporary philosophical conversations. Contemporary philosophers and cultural critics do not take into account the productive struggle over ideas that occurred between Paul and those to whom he wrote, and they assume that people's experience of an urgent expectation of the Parousia or appearance of Christ allowed for some sort of individualized spiritual transformation that nonetheless had no concrete social or political effects in the world.

1 Corinthians 8–10

Food Offered to Idols, Ethnicity, and Identity

The Text in Its Ancient Context

Paul had said that the Corinthians are still "infants" (*nēpioi*) and "people of the flesh" (*sarkikoi* or *sarkinoi*, 3:1). Chapters 5-10 provide examples of the practical ethical outworkings of Paul's chastisement. While chapters 5-7 touched on issues of practices of the *sōma* that had particularly to do with sex and marriage, chapters 8-10 focus on practices regarding food and transformations in ethnic identity that occur for those in Christ.

In 1 Cor. 10:25, Paul uses the word *makellon*, a *hapax legomenon* (a word that appears only once) in New Testament literature (Cadbury): "Eat whatever is sold in the meat market without raising any question on the ground of conscience" (1 Cor. 10:25). The location of the *makellon* (an area primarily for selling meat and fish) in Roman Corinth is unclear, although fragmentary epigraphic evidence confirms that there was a *makellon* at Corinth (Cadbury, 139; Nabers; Kent, n. 321; West, n. 124; Nasrallah forthcoming). Although not all meat in antiquity was sacrificial meat, the markets were locations where trade and religion converged, along with the sale of meat (Ruyt). Divinities were honored there in the Roman imperial period, especially in the central, usually round building (Ruyt; Nabers).

In chapters 8–10, Paul offers somewhat contradictory advice about the eating of meat in sacred precincts or from the market. In chapter 8, on the one hand, he suggests that one shouldn't eat it (in particular not in sacred precincts, *en eidōleiō*), lest one offend the conscience of a "weak" brother or sister. In chapter 10, on the other hand, he indicates that one shouldn't ask about the origins of the sacrificial food (*hierothyton*)—one can go ahead and eat it. Two principles seem to dominate: first, a set of philosophical-theological slogans, likely the Corinthians' own: we know that there is one God, that idols don't really exist, and that the earth is the Lord's and everything in it; in sum: God trumps all, and it doesn't matter what you eat. Second, and in tension with the first, we find a social issue: think about your sibling's conscience, and don't offend your brother or sister by eating sacrificial food. With regard to eating and drinking in Corinth, we can also consider the question of the meals shared by those in Christ; we know that Paul considered these to be handled badly, and his comments indicate that some were likely poor and were certainly hungry (see below on 1 Cor. 11:17–34; e.g., Stowers 2011a). Debates about food in Gal. 2:11–13, in which Paul accuses Cephas of sitting at table with gentiles, then separating from them when some from James (brother of Jesus) came to visit, likely had to do with kashrut or Jewish dietary laws more generally, while the discussion in 1 Corinthians 8-10 seems to have to do more specifically with food associated with sacrifice and sacred precincts.

The Corinthians in Christ were familiar with the intimate connection between food, community, and cult. Meals were eaten in sanctuaries at Corinth. The Asklepieion near the Lerna Fountain at Corinth has some rooms that seem to have functioned for dining. In addition, excavations have revealed fish bones, lentils, and casserole dishes in the sanctuary of Demeter and Kore on the Acrocorinth, which had several structures for dining even in the Roman period (Bookidis and Stroud; Økland). Not only meat but also other sorts of food were sometimes sacrificial, and if not sacrificial, still sacralized by their consumption within sacred precincts (Ekroth), yet not all meat was sacrificial meat (Naiden). Yet Paul tries to convince the Corinthians that the commodity could be drained of its religious force (see discussions in Still; Gooch; Stowers 2011a).

If we ask how various participants in the Corinthian *ekklēsia* would have heard Paul's injunction to "eat whatever is sold in the meat market," we recognize, aided by archaeological materials, that the conditions in antiquity were such that slaves, free, or freedpersons entered into a market that was religiously marked to purchase goods that may or may not have been religiously marked. In addition, literary evidence often depicts slaves sent to the market to purchase food (e.g., *Life of Aesop*). Hearers of 1 Corinthians would have found it difficult to think of *hierothyton* as neutral food, or of their mandated or voluntary entrance into the meat market as religiously neutral. The commodity in question was tagged by religion, whether or not it is called *hierothyton* ("sacred offering") or *eidōlothyton* ("idol" or "image offering"). The food, the eating of it, and the market space are all marked by religious practice and affiliation.

Spliced into the conversations about food and idolatry in chapters 8 and 10 is Paul's own assertion regarding food, one's right (*exousia*), freedom, and his identity in chapter 9. (We also saw how chapters 1-4 contrapuntally treat wisdom and Paul's role within the community.) "Am I not free?!" Paul begins chapter 9. While Paul presents himself at the beginning of 1 Corinthians (and at its end) as an apostle, not slave of Christ (as in Rom. 1:1), Paul here presents himself as analogous to one "employed in the temple" (9:13). Such religious experts were not necessarily (only) high-status priests but also temple slaves and/or public slaves in the employ of the temple (Shaner). Wondering about his own finances, Paul refers to temple religious specialists eating from the altar. This image is easily skimmed over as an odd metaphor, so that we can get to the meat (!) of Paul's self-description in 9:19–23, but it is a crucial tie to the themes of chapters 7-8 and 10-11. In chapters 7-8, real slavery and freedom are at stake, as is the question of eating meat from the temple. In chapters 10-11, eating *hierothyton* is again an issue, and by the end of chapter 11 the *ekklēsia* at Corinth is criticized for how it does its eating and drinking.

What is at stake in these verses is Paul's identity as an apostle, what authority (*exousia*, 9:12b) he has in the community at Corinth, and his wage (*misthos*, 9:18). Paul responds to this by proudly stating that he is a shape-shifter. "For though I am free with respect to all, I have made myself a slave to all, so that I might win more of them. To the Jews I became as a Jew . . . To those outside the law I became as one outside the law . . . To the weak I became weak . . . I have become all things to all people, that I might by all means save some" (9:19–22). The passage is confounding if we look for Paul's biography or an insight into his psychology; we should read it instead as part of Paul's *ēthos*—the rhetorical strategy by which a speaker both defines himself and does so in a way that he hopes will draw the audience's sympathy.

Paul twice pauses in his arguments in chapters 8-9 to refer to Jewish Scripture. In 8:6, he offers a remix of the Shema, the Jewish claim in Scripture and prayer that the Lord is one (Deut. 6:4), expanded by a reference to "one Lord, Jesus Christ," perhaps quoting a common teaching of early Christ-communities and perhaps also sparking, for the Corinthians, the idea of Stoic monotheism (Thiselton, 635–37). That is, Jews were not the only ones in antiquity who argued for one God; some who followed Greek and Roman religions also thought that there was one true God, and various local manifestations or ways of imagining aspects of that God. In chapter 9, speaking of the issue of wage, Paul offers an allegorical interpretation of Deut. 25:4, insisting, in what I think must be a comic tone, that "You shall not muzzle an ox while it is treading out the grain" is a Mosaic statement for "our sake": in the midst of a chapter about Paul's own identity, he briefly takes on the identity of an ox. From these references and from the beginning of chapter 10, we can deduce that the Corinthians understood references to Jewish tradition and that they were a largely gentile community, undergoing an ethnic-religious transformation toward a Jewishness rooted in faith in Christ.

At the beginning of chapter 10, Paul reprises the theme of food and idolatry using the exodus story. "I don't want you to be ignorant, brothers and sisters," he writes—again, a reference to who is in the know—"that our fathers were all under the cloud and all passed through the sea, and all were baptized into Moses in the cloud and in the sea, and all ate the same spiritual food and all drank the same spiritual drink. For they drank from the spiritual rock which followed them, and the rock was Christ" (10:1–4). The passage was perhaps surprising to the Corinthians as they recalled their ethnic change. It asserts that the paternity of those to whom Paul writes is derived from Moses, despite the fact that he later writes "when you were gentiles" (12:2)—that is, from the *ethnē*, or nations, that are precisely not Jews. The story of the exodus through the sea is framed in terms of baptism. This passage reminds us again that the Corinthians considered baptism to be a key ritual, perhaps one that transformed identity, community, and possibilities for present and future. Baptism, as we know from what is likely a pre-Pauline baptismal formula found in Gal. 3:28, included the phrase "neither Jew nor Greek." Here, as in Gal. 3:29, Paul reinforces the idea that baptism does not lead to an ethnically neutral state or to participation in a third or "new race," as some Christians would later assert (*Diogn.*1.1; Buell), but to being incorporated within the stories, covenants, promises, and responsibilities of God's people, the Jews.

Here Paul offers a midrash on the exodus story that may trade on and shift other interpretations of exodus familiar to those at Corinth. In a roughly contemporaneous text, the Wisdom of Solomon, Wisdom herself leads the people through the sea.

> A holy people and blameless race wisdom delivered from a nation of oppressors. . . . She brought them over the Red Sea, and led them through deep waters; . . . wisdom opened the mouth of the dumb, and made the tongues of babes speak clearly. . . . When they thirsted they called upon thee [Wisdom], and water was given them out of flinty rock, and slaking of thirst from hard stone. (Wis. 10:15, 18, 21; 11:4)

The accounts in 1 Corinthians and the Wisdom of Solomon differ in various ways. The latter is a celebration of Jewish identity over against "the nations" and "the ungodly"; the former brings the nations into a Jewish lineage. The Wisdom of Solomon celebrates Wisdom; Paul may substitute Christ for Wisdom. The triumph of the story of the Wisdom of Solomon becomes a warning in 1 Corinthians: the latter tells the story of the exodus as a warning concerning idolatry, instruction, and trial or temptation, rather than a celebration as we find in the Wisdom of Solomon. Given what we learned in chapters 1-4 of the importance of wisdom/Wisdom to the Corinthian *ekklēsia*, we may reasonably wonder whether Paul is trying to shift the importance of this hypostatized figure in the community at Corinth.

The Text in the Interpretive Tradition

In 10:26, Paul cites from Ps. 24:1 a kind of cosmological-philosophical slogan: "The earth is the Lord's, and everything in it." Such a way of thinking means that *anything*, even foodstuffs usually considered questionable, taboo, or forbidden due to dietary laws, is reframed as "the Lord's" and is thus acceptable. We find concern about this issue also in Gal. 2:11, framed in terms of Jews eating with gentiles. Written approximately fifty years later, Acts 10 reframes the fundamental insight in terms of dietary law and gives to Peter, not Paul, the vision (literally) that God says he may "kill and eat" all things (10:13). Acts adopts this probably earlier story to provide Peter with the insight that he can travel to the household of Cornelius the gentile, since "God has shown me that I should not call anyone profane or unclean" (10:28). Some recent scholars have argued that the canonical Acts of the Apostles knows Paul's letters and self-presentation, even if Acts presents Paul in quite a different light, as a tremendous speaker rather than one who is weak (Pervo). Acts 10 presents a *different* tradition from Paul's own in 1 Corinthians 8-10 with regard to eating and idolatry and relations with gentiles, so it is an "interpretive context" for Paul's letter in the loosest sense. But it is important to recognize that the community in Christ, whether in the time of Paul or in the century thereafter, picks up Jewish interpretive traditions that declare the Mosaic laws to be allegorizations of *people*, rather than literal injunctions about what to eat. For example, the *Letter of Aristeas* depicts a figure named Eleazar the high priest, who argues that Moses' true aim is *dikaiosynē* ("righteousness" or "justice"), and so Mosaic dietary law is to be interpreted with each animal as a symbol that corresponds to human ethical behavior (see Svebakken, 111–12).

First Corinthians 10:25 is used quite differently by Clement in second-century-CE Alexandria, who employs it in a larger section on eating, both to enjoin people not to "abolish social intercourse" but also to shun "daintiness . . . we are to partake of few and necessary things." A string of citations from 1 Corinthians leads Clement to mark his intended audience as fairly wealthy, since his conclusions have to do both with the host and with moderation at a luxurious table: "We are to partake of what is set before us, as becomes a Christian, out of respect to him who has invited us, by a harmless and moderate participation in the social meeting; regarding the sumptuousness of what is put on the table as a matter of indifference, despising the dainties, as after a little destined to perish" (*Strom.* 4.15). In the community at Corinth and elsewhere, food, status, economic access, and religious practice were intertwined issues. Maybe you aren't what you eat, but you are formed by those with whom you eat.

The Text in Contemporary Discussion

Paul presents himself as a shape-shifter in 1 Corinthians 9, as "all things to all people." In other passages in his letters, he presents himself as nurse (1 Thess. 2:7), as father coming with a stick (1 Cor. 4:15–21), as someone having ecstatic experiences (2 Cor. 12:1–11), and as prisoner (Phil. 1:13–14), among many other self-portraits. Paul's presentation in 1 Corinthians, as well as these other self-portraits, has informed two responses. First, Paul offers a self so complex that students of his letters struggle to define his intention: Who *was* Paul? What was his frame of mind? This has led to a scholarly obsession with declaring Paul a hero (often a liberative or postcolonial hero, resisting the Roman Empire and bringing egalitarian community) or a betrayer of Christ's message (from the Pseudo-Clementine literature to Thomas Jefferson and beyond: Johnson-DeBaufre and Nasrallah). A better approach would be (1) to take into account the rhetorical nature of Paul's statements: he is not describing himself, but portraying himself to various communities for various reasons; (2) to consider whether our ideas of authorship and intention might not match those held in antiquity; and (3) to focus not only on Paul as hero but on the broad spectrum of early communities in Christ as well.

Second, some scholars of the past decades have interpreted Paul's shape-shifting in the context of the "new perspective" on Paul, placing Paul as a Jew negotiating his newly Jewish identity *in Christ* in the midst of the diversity within Judaism in the first century CE. They demonstrate that Paul has not invented a new religion, but stands alongside other Jews who try to make a way for gentiles to come into covenant with God.

1 Corinthians 11:2–34

Veiling and Eating

The Text in Its Ancient Context

In chapter 9, Paul pointed to his own identity as shape-shifter; by the end of chapter 10, he emphasizes that his readers should do all to the glory of God and give no offense to "either Jew or Greeks or the *ekklēsia* of God," even as he himself seeks to please the many. Paul enjoins his audience here to "Be imitators of me, as I am of Christ" (11:1; see also 4:16). The pattern set up in this verse (Christ-Paul-participants in the *ekklēsia*) echoes throughout the following verses, even as the powerful political language of imitation echoes elsewhere in this letter and others (Castelli).

An initial commendation to the community for remembering him and what he has "handed down" quickly shifts to a correction of practices of prayer and prophecy. Paul begins by setting a hierarchy of "headship"—God, Christ, man, wife. This hierarchy undergirds his insistence that a man praying or prophesying should do so with head uncovered, while a woman doing so must cover her head. As Antoinette Clark Wire has shown, Paul then proceeds to offer several disparate logics for his insistence on such a practice. Although scholars have long tried to discover the causes of such an injunction—Does Paul promote Jewish women's practices of head-veiling? Does he criticize "pagan" women's loose hair and/or prophetic chaos leading to Dionysian-like abandon for women?—none is convincing, largely because we cannot know for certain the variety of veiling practices in Roman Corinth. We do know that Roman men *and* women covered their heads when engaged in pious practices, as we see in a statue of Octavian found at Corinth; were his right hand preserved, we would see it pouring a libation to the gods (see also Oster).

If we cannot fix a social context that explains Paul's injunction, we can glean several things about prayer and prophecy in the community at Corinth. First, men and women alike were praying and prophesying; as we think about the letter as a whole, we see that wisdom and spiritual gifts are key to the community (11:1–4, 12–14). Second, Paul wishes to change this practice in some way, perhaps especially through insisting on women's veiling and grounding this practice in a logic of women's subordination to men. Third, given the scattershot of logics he offers, it is likely that he is aware he faces a tough crowd, for whom only one reason for his argument will not suffice. Paul argues according to cosmology and creation: man as God's image and glory; woman as glory of the man; the Genesis 2 story that woman was made from man, with a concessive realization that men are born from women in verse 12. He argues according to "the angels," either indicating that the Corinthians understood angels to be present in their community practices and/or that he was alluding to the danger of angels' attraction to human women, as is hinted at in the biblical reference to angelic intercourse with female humans (Gen. 6:1–2; Wire; BeDuhn). Paul argues based on the logic of propriety (11:13), from nature (11:14), and from general practice in the *ekklēsiai* (11:16).

Paul proceeds to another practice that has to do with Corinthians' gathering (11:17–34): that of eating and drinking. When they gather to eat, he says, they do not engage in "the Lord's supper" (11:20). One concern, according to the text, is that "those who have nothing" (11:22) are humiliated. From Paul's perspective, something in meal practices has broken down. Scholars have speculated that perhaps this breakdown has to do with social status: some have access to food or the ability to come when they wish, leaving out or disregarding others with less status, such as slaves. Paul's final word is to "wait" lest condemnation fall (11:34).

Paul's discussion of what he "received from the Lord" about the supper is the earliest evidence we have of such a practice; although the traditions contained in the Gospels may be earlier, the Gospels themselves postdate the writing of Paul's letters. The meal is grounded with a historical etiology ("on the night he was handed over," 11:23): it is understood as a repetition of the practices of that first supper. The eschatological aspect of the meal is highlighted, as it is a proclamation of the death of the Lord "until he comes." For Paul, the Lord's Supper has potential dangers associated with it; interpreters influenced by the anthropology of religion have noted Paul's attribution of quasi-magical properties to the supper, since it can cause weakness, illness, and death if misused (11:30).

Those in Christ were not the only ones to gather at meals or to be warned about their behavior while doing so. Contemporaneous associations were well known for their practices of gathering to eat and to celebrate a god, and for regulating those gatherings. The second-century Iobacchoi inscription found in Athens, for instance, regulates participation and membership in their association to honor the god Bacchus (Dionysus) and states fines for poor behavior while in a gathering together (IG II^2 1368=PHI 3584) as well as the financial contributions necessary to participate in the meal (Ascough, et al.).

Comments regarding meal practices in 1 Corinthians 11 should make us wonder not only about the ritual nature of the meal but also about food and hunger in the community. The majority of the population of the Roman Empire was poor (recent hypotheses extend from 68 to 99 percent), with poverty defined in this way by Peter Garnsey and Greg Woolf: "the poor are those living at or near subsistence level, whose prime concern it is to obtain the minimum food, shelter, and clothing necessary to sustain life, whose lives are dominated by the struggle for physical survival" (Garnsey and Woolf, 153; Meggitt). Various famines occurred in mid-first-century Greece and the Greek East, including perhaps one at Corinth in the early 50s CE (Winter, 6, 216–25). Corinth's economy depended on trade, and the city and its environs could not supply enough food for its urban population (Williams, 31–33, 38; Strabo, *Geog.* 8.6.23).

The Text in the Interpretive Tradition

Paul's assertion that women should be veiled when praying or prophesying and his arguments supporting this change in practice may have met with instant controversy. It also created controversy in the late second or early third century, as evidenced in the writings of Tertullian. The North African writer is famous for his pithy statement that "you [women] are the devil's gateway" (*On the Apparel of Women* 1.1). In *On the Veiling of Virgins*, Tertullian discusses 1 Corinthians 11 and the way in which it is being interpreted in his day. Some, he indicates, argue from 1 Corinthians 11 that, while women should veil while praying or prophesying, virgins should not; thus, virgins in those Christian communities in North Africa remain unveiled when they gather with others in church. These interpreters, Tertullian disgustedly says, ground their argument in Paul's statement about the unmarried woman being concerned about the affairs of the Lord, while the married woman worries about worldly affairs and how to please her husband (1 Cor. 7:34; Tertullian, *Virg.* 4.4).

Tertullian cites 1 Cor. 11:3 and its language of man as head of woman—a term in Greek that can also be translated "wife," but which Tertullian insists must be understood as a general classificatory term under which female virgin falls as a particular instance of "woman." He continues to argue that virgin women should also be veiled by appealing to the assertion in 1 Cor. 14:34–35 that women should be silent in the assembly. Is a virgin, he wonders acerbically, something of a third sex (*Virg.*7.2), which can escape such regulations? In the end, he supports his argumentation by referring to a vision of a woman in his community to whom an angel appeared, rapping on her bare neck and sarcastically suggesting that she expose more of her body (*Virg.*17.6). The issue of women and veiling in religious practice is a long-standing one, and some among earliest Christians argued strongly for women's veiling in religious community.

The Text in Contemporary Discussion

Scholars today debate whether the Greek *kephalē* in 1 Cor. 11:3 should be translated "head" (as in RSV) or "source"; the latter might allow for a nonhierarchical interpretation of the passage, with the term "source" indicating the order of creation. At stake is the role of women in Christian community. Does 1 Corinthians provide a biblical foundation for the idea of women's subordination to men, especially with regard to women's roles in religious leadership in Christian ministry?

Mimi Haddad, president of Christians for Biblical Equality, along with many who participate in the organization, argues that 1 Corinthians 11 refers to the order of creation. Paul states in 1 Cor. 11:8–9, 11–12, that, despite the order of creation (man first, then woman, according to Genesis 2), men are now born from women. Haddad and others cite this as evidence of Paul's recognition of the roles of both sexes and the interdependence of men and women. She concludes: "Rather, in Christ both males and females are equal heirs of God's New Covenant community. Both are born of the Spirit, and both are gifted for leadership which is first and foremost service" (Haddad).

Haddad's perspective is one among many who debate whether Paul argued for women's egalitarian status in assemblies in Christ or argued for women's subordination (Elliott). Other feminist approaches would emphasize the clear role of women in the earliest Jesus movement, from accounts that Mary Magdalene was the first to greet Jesus after his resurrection to Paul's own list of women who were coworkers and even a woman apostle in Romans 16. Still others would add that the texts we associate with earliest Christianity, like all writing, are rhetorically constructed in order to persuade, and would ask why Paul here insists on a hierarchy that is in part gendered, while elsewhere in Paul's writings and other texts we find evidence of egalitarian tendencies in the early *ekklēsiai*.

1 Corinthians 12:1–26

Being the Body of Christ

The Text in Its Ancient Context

Paul introduces the topic with the statement, "Now concerning spiritual gifts [or "spiritual things," *pneumatika*], brothers and sisters, I do not want you to be uninformed" (12:1). This statement may have been a surprise to those at Corinth who heard these words: with their interest in wisdom and knowledge, the Corinthians likely understood themselves to be quite well informed about spiritual gifts. The Corinthians, with their interest in *pneumatika*, were on the cutting edge of an emerging medical and philosophical debate in the first and second centuries, including medical debates over whether "spirit" runs through the blood and philosophical debates about the materiality of *pneuma*. From the fourth to the first centuries BCE, terms etymologically related to *pneumatika* are found approximately thirty-six times in extant literary writings. In writings from the first century CE, however, we find at least 104 uses of the term, and in the second century CE, a shocking 990 uses; a good many of these are Christian, emerging because of discussion of 1 Corinthians (Nasrallah 2003).

Nevertheless, even as Paul likely mirrors the Corinthians' own interest in and discussions of *pneumatika* and their participation in a broader cultural fascination with the topic of *pneuma*, he asserts that they do not understand spiritual gifts particularly well. He ranks spiritual gifts and seeks to reconfigure the importance of prophecy and glossolalia in the Corinthian community.

Paul embeds his ranking of spiritual gifts in a discussion of the body. First Corinthians is full of advice on the discipline and control of the individual body in relation to the "one body" of the *ekklēsia*. Paul uses the image of many members making up that one body (12:12–27). He uses the term *sōma* in two primary ways. The first is the *sōma* as the individual body, which can be transformed (1 Cor. 15:35–50) and, as we recall, can be bought (6:20; 7:23a). Paul folds this image of body into an image of "one body" as community ("For just as the body is one and has many members, and all the members of the body, though many, are one body, so it is with Christ," 12:12), joking that the foot shouldn't compete with the hand nor the ear complain that it isn't an eye. This language of one body derives from the political discourse of the day.

The image of "one body" and the idea of communal benefit are powerful tools of deliberative rhetoric, and present an argument that few would want to dispute. Who wants to damage the common body? The first-century-CE Stoic philosopher Epictetus enjoins: "you are a citizen of the world, and a part of it," and urges his hearers "to treat nothing as a matter of private profit . . . but to act like the foot or the hand, which, if they had the faculty of reason and understood the constitution of nature, would never exercise choice or desire in any other way but by reference to the whole" (*Diatr.* 2.10.1–4 [Oldfather, 275]. By the second century, the cities of Asia Minor aggressively minted coinage representing *homonoia*, the unity between these bodies politic, even as at the same time they fiercely competed with each other to secure Roman imperial attention and funds (Price; Kampmann).

Along with the rhetoric of one body, Paul employs the political language of "general benefit," often employed in deliberative rhetoric, to persuade the audience: all spiritual gifts must be for the general benefit (*to sympheron*, 12:7; Mitchell 1991). Paul's statement that all spiritual gifts are from the same spirit (12:11), moreover, further underscores his emphasis on unity and sameness over and against or in the midst of the diversity of spiritual gifts.

Paul's emphasis in chapter 12 on the common benefit and one body reorders and marginalizes those spiritual gifts that are connected to wisdom and knowledge, and that the Corinthians may have most valued. The general list of spiritual gifts in verses 8–10 is ranked in

12:28: "And God has appointed in the church first apostles, second prophets, third teachers; then deeds of power, then gifts of healing, forms of assistance, forms of leadership, various kinds of tongues." While 1 Cor. 12:14–26 argues for the significance of every member of the body, both the "weaker" and those given more "honor," this argument is undercut by the ranking and ordering of *pneumatika* in 12:28. This ranking erodes the emphasis on wisdom and knowledge—and concomitantly glossolalia and prophecy, gifts the Corinthians held dear. Paul admits the importance of prophets, but subordinates them to apostles; he also disaggregates prophecy from glossolalia, and ranks the latter last, perhaps as part of his strategy of challenging the Corinthians' understanding of Wisdom. After all, she was associated with eloquence and speech: "wisdom opened the mouth of the dumb, and made the tongues of babes speak clearly" (Wis. 10:21). Even infants (recall Paul's accusation in 3:1) benefit from Wisdom.

The Text in the Interpretive Tradition

Christian communities have long struggled with questions of how the divine is manifest in different historical periods. Some early Christians believed that the Spirit and its gifts were relegated to a past time; the beginning of the *Martyrdom of Perpetua and Felicitas* (1.4) argues that new witnesses may still be found, and indeed may be greater than past ones: "Let those then who would restrict the power of the one Spirit to times and seasons look to this: the more recent events should be considered the greater, being later than those of old, and this is a consequence of the extraordinary graces promised for the last stage of time" (Musurillo). This is followed by a citation of Acts 2:17/Joel 2:28, which refers to the Lord pouring out "my spirit upon all flesh." The passage continues with allusions to ideas of Spirit, community benefit, and distribution of gifts also found in 1 Corinthians: "So too we hold in honour and acknowledge not only new prophecies but new visions as well, according to the promise. And we consider all the other functions of the Holy Spirit as intended for the good of the Church; for the same

Spirit has been sent to distribute all his gifts to all, as the Lord apportions to everyone" (1.5; Musurillo).

In earliest Christianity, some groups celebrated new manifestations of the Spirit. This was certainly the case for those who edited and used the *Martyrdom of Perpetua and Felicitas*, a community that may have been associated with the prophetic renewal movement, sometimes called Montanism, that arose in Asia Minor in the late second century CE and flourished for some time around the Mediterranean basin. Of course, such prophetic renewal movements were not limited to ancient times, but can be found in a figure like Joachim of Fiore in the twelfth century or the movement, sparked at Azusa Street in Los Angeles in the early twentieth century, that came to be called Pentecostalism.

The Text in Contemporary Discussion

We find a comparable phenomenon in the Shakers or the United Society of Believers in Christ's Second Coming, which began in the mid-eighteenth century and was characterized by women's leadership, ideas of the equality of the sexes, an understanding of an unfolding Parousia or appearance of Christ, and ecstatic experiences of spiritual gifts, including speaking in tongues. The community was known for "shaking" and speaking in tongues and prophesying. The 1816 biography of one key leader, Ann Lee, talks about the gifts of the Holy Ghost and the current time when people can be filled "with visions, revelations and gifts of God" (Bishop and Wells, v; 7). Although much of their understanding of revelation is grounded in interpretations of the book of Revelation, some Shaker writings combine references to Saul of Tarsus with reference to gifts (and 1 Cor. 2:11) in order to argue for a new, Spirit-filled dispensation (see the 1848 edition of *A Summary View of the Millennial Church, or United Society of Believers, Commonly Called Shakers* 5.5). The Spirit's working was sometimes manifest in "gift drawings" and in "gift music" (Morin).

Debate about dispensations of time and the Spirit have not ceased. Global Pentecostalism, in all its variegated forms, is a growing force in

Christianity, especially in the so-called two-thirds world, while academic engagement with such ideas is ongoing (*The Journal of Pentecostal Studies*; J. K. A. Smith; Miller and Yamamori). Different Christian communities use the very same text, 1 Corinthians, to argue for the effervescence of the Spirit's inbreaking in community *and* to argue, to the contrary, that true Christian community gathers in a unified way in which all speech is comprehensible and the use of tongues is barred.

1 Corinthians 12:27–13:13
Love and the Ranking of Charismata

The Text in Its Ancient Context

Chapter 13 seems like a digression because some of these materials are pre-Pauline, a kind of aretalogy of love derived from Jewish wisdom traditions (Conzelmann, 218). Yet its contents are intimately linked to the foregoing and following chapters on *pneumatika*: the themes of prophecy and tongues in particular, and the question of who is a spiritual person in general.

Chapter 13 begins by citing spiritual gifts significant at Corinth, but then relativizes their importance: "If I speak in the tongues of mortals and of angels, but do not have love, I am a noisy gong or a clanging cymbal. And if I have prophetic powers, and understand all mysteries and all knowledge, and if I have all faith, so as to remove mountains, but do not have love, I am nothing" (13:1–2). Paul emphasizes that these three things the Corinthians value (tongues, prophecy, faith) will all pass away, while "love never ends" (13:8). Returning to the theme of perfection (*to teleion*) raised in chapter 2, in which Paul contrasted the perfect person or initiate with the faulty Corinthians, Paul insists, "Our knowledge is imperfect and our prophecy is imperfect; but when the perfect comes, the imperfect will pass away" (13:9–10). Using the metaphors of being an infant and of gazing into a dim mirror, 1 Corinthians 13 emphasizes the immaturity and partialness of any sort of present knowledge and wisdom.

Verses 4–8a may present a pre-Pauline aretalogy—that is, a list of virtues or qualities—of love that is used to relativize the importance of wisdom in the Corinthian community. Aretalogies of Wisdom (as well as of Isis, who has qualities similar to Wisdom) are well known from the ancient world, and it is possible that the Corinthians knew these and celebrated Wisdom in their midst. First Corinthians 13 may seek to redirect the community's interest in wisdom by celebrating love instead, just as chapters 1-4 attempted to upend expectations about what true wisdom and knowledge are.

The Text in the Interpretive Tradition

Later Christian commentators connected Paul's comment, "If I deliver my body to be burned, but have not love, I gain nothing" (1 Cor. 13:3), to martyrdom. (Note that here lies one of the text-critical debates of 1 Corinthians: is the word "burn" or "boast" original to Paul's letter? They differ by only one letter in Greek.) In late second-century Alexandria, Clement argued: "You see that martyrdom for love's sake is taught" (*Strom.* 4.7). To celebrate the idea of the glory of a noble death, Clement cites Pindar, Aeschylus, Heraclitus, the words of Indian sages meeting Alexander the Great, and even Plato's *Republic*, among other sources. His discussion culminates with an argument about Christians displaying a true understanding of death for true love, a death that leads to glory, in a mix of Pauline verses from 1 Corinthians 13 about enduring love and 1 Cor. 4:9–13 about apostolic suffering. In heresiological debates, the verse is used to denigrate Christians with whom one disagrees. For instance, Tertullian argues that if Praxeas's body had been burned (in martyrdom)—Praxeas being another Christian whom Tertullian considered heretical—it would have profited him nothing since he did not have the love of God (*Prax.* 1.4).

First Corinthians 13 had a powerful afterlife as well in Augustine's *On Christian Doctrine*. All Scripture should be interpreted in light of "faith, hope, and love" while knowledge and prophecies fall away. Even a mistaken interpretation of Scripture, if it builds up love, argued

Augustine, still goes in the right direction, even if the interpreter needs to be put correctly on the right path of interpretation (*On Christian Doctrine* 1.36–40). A person who has "faith, hope, and love" (1 Cor. 13:13) does not even need Scripture, except to instruct others (*On Christian Doctrine* 1.39). Dale Martin powerfully suggests that this principle of interpretation be applied to passages by Paul and those writing in his name that are used to condemn what some might today call homosexuality, especially in view of the quite different sex-gender system of the ancient world (Martin 2006, 49–50).

The Text in Contemporary Discussion

In a sermon given on November 4, 1956, in Montgomery, Alabama, Martin Luther King Jr. delivered "Paul's Letter to American Christians." In it, "Paul" wonders at the "fascinating and astounding advances that you have made in the scientific realm" but states, "It seems to me that your moral progress lags behind your scientific progress" (M. L. King, 415), quoting Henry David Thoreau to support his argument. He offers an economic critique of capitalism's excesses, while arguing that America cannot turn to communism. He critiques American Protestantism, Roman Catholicism, and segregation in American society, particularly in the churches. He concludes by calling love the "most durable power in the world," and declares that it is "at bottom the heartbeat of the moral cosmos" (M. L. King, 420). He reaches this conclusion by interpreting 1 Corinthians 13, arguing that American Christians' "eloquence of articulate speech," "heights of academic achievement," and philanthropy are nothing if devoid of love: "I must bring my writing to a close now. Timothy is waiting to deliver this letter, and I must take leave for another church. But just before leaving, I must say to you, as I said to the church at Corinth, that I still believe that love is the most durable power in the world" (419). Martin Luther King, Jr., uses 1 Corinthians 13 to offer a cultural critique and to navigate the troubled waters of American politics by foregrounding a love that expels inequalities, whether of economics, race, or education.

1 Corinthians 14:1–40

Spiritual Gifts and Building up Community

The Text in Its Ancient Context

In 1 Cor. 14:1, Paul picks up the themes of the previous chapters and continues to work out his arguments about spiritual gifts, especially prophecy and glossolalia. "Pursue love," Paul insists, referring back to the contents of chapter 13; and "strive for the spiritual gifts," reminding his readers/hearers of chapter 12, "especially that you may prophesy." This last phrase reminds us that Paul highlights prophecy over against tongues. Paul may have invented this division; it is possible that the Corinthian community had not categorized and ranked the *pneumatika* received at baptism.

Paul offers a series of arguments that deconstruct the importance of tongues. These arguments hinge on the concepts of "building up" (*oikodomē*)—as we recall, a key term in political rhetoric of the first century—and intelligibility. In 1 Corinthians 14, by his own admission, Paul seeks to rein in tongues, which are a primary means of accessing the divine and divine knowledge: "For those who speak in a tongue do not speak to other people but to God; for nobody understands them, since they are speaking mysteries in the spirit" (14:2). Yet Paul admits in 1 Corinthians 14 that he too speaks in tongues. He thus asserts that he can match the high status of any Corinthian who exhibits glossolalia, but chooses not to. By the time of the writing of 2 Corinthians 12, Paul feels forced to argue again on the Corinthians' terms, especially over against the "super-apostles" with their spiritual gifts. Thus Paul circuitously talks about his own "visions and revelations" (2 Cor. 12:1). In his famous "fool's speech," Paul insists that the Corinthians' resistance to him has compelled him to enter into a sort of performance competition where he must demonstrate that he too has experienced rich charismatic experiences.

Because of passages like 1 Corinthians 12–14, because of Paul's discussion of his own ecstatic experience in 2 Corinthians 10–12, and because of Paul's references to bearing Christ's body or to having the spirit of God (7:40), some have understood Paul as a mystic (Schweitzer) or a shaman (Ashton). Others have pointed to spirit-possession as an important characteristic of the religious lives of Corinthians (J. Z. Smith; Mount).

The Text in the Interpretive Tradition

First Corinthians 14:33b–34, with its comments on women (or, less likely, wives; the Greek *gynaikes* can mean either) being silent in the *ekklēsia*, clearly raised issues for later Christians. This can be seen from the way in which various manuscripts treat the verses. We have none of Paul's "autographs," or original manuscripts; thus variations from text to text in the manuscripts we do have often indicate early Christian interpretations of those now-lost origins. In several manuscripts, verses 34–35 are displaced to after verse 40; in other manuscripts, including the early P[46] (third century), these verses appear as following verse 33 (Thiselton, 1148). Some have hypothesized that because this text "wanders," it may not have been original, but a scribal gloss (Fee), but Wire demonstrates that the "wandering" nature of the passage traces back only to one manuscript, thus strengthening the argument that this is *not* an interpolation (Thiselton, 1148–49). While Paul mentions prominent women leaders in the earliest *ekklēsiai* (see Romans 16), in 1 Corinthians 11 he also offers a subordinationist logic for women's veiling. In addition, that passage, as well as 1 Corinthians 15, relies on the account in Genesis 2 of man's creation first, and woman's creation from man; it may be that the Corinthians (as with other, later Christian communities) relied instead on the idea in Gen. 1:27 that God created the human in God's image, "male and female God created them." We cannot know Paul's intentions, and his letters offer contradictory indications regarding the role of women in earliest Christian communities. What we can know is that Paul's letters indicate women's leadership and voice in earliest in-Christ communities, and both his support for and ambivalence about this phenomenon. His arguments for veiling and women's silence indicate that they were praying and prophesying in community unveiled, on the one hand, and that they were vocal in the community, on the other. Looking in 1 Corinthians and to other texts, especially Romans 16, we find a panoply of women in communication with Paul and leading in communities. Those who draw from Paul's letters the justification for subordinating women's leadership in worship have grounds to do so, and those who use Paul's letters to argue for women's leadership have grounds to do so as well.

The Text in Contemporary Discussion

The story of the origins of Pentecostalism at Azusa Street in Los Angeles, California, is replete with references to Acts 1-2 and the story of *heteroglossia*—speaking in other languages—in those passages. References to 1 Corinthians 12-14, with its emphasis on *glossolalia*, speaking in tongues, are puzzlingly less utilized, perhaps precisely because of how Paul cites his own speaking in tongues yet also downgrades and relativizes the importance of this spiritual gift among others.

One contemporary Pentecostal treatment of 1 Corinthians 14 comes in a sermon by Rev. David Yonggi Cho, pastor of the Yoido Full Gospel Church in South Korea (Myung and Hong). In 2007, this Pentecostal church claimed approximately a million members. In a sermon titled "The Benefits of Speaking in Tongues," preached on February 15, 2009, Cho began by narrating the origins of global Pentecostalism at Azusa Street. His sermon, grounded in 1 Cor. 14:18 ("I thank God that I speak in tongues more than all of you"), emphasizes the ongoing importance of this spiritual gift. Cho provides five reasons for speaking in tongues to encourage his audience to continue in the practice. He argues that speaking in tongues benefits the individual, who can pray in the spirit with the help of the Paraclete (the term used for the Holy Spirit in John's Gospel). It allows for prayers to well up when the person praying is sufficiently despairing that she or he cannot find a way to pray. It allows for all-night prayer vigils since, without the Holy Spirit, Christians would be unequal to the task of praying all night. Speaking in tongues, he asserts, can cast out a devil, and the Christian who speaks in tongues needs no psychologist as tongues have a healing function. Speaking in tongues, Cho further states, can calm nightmares and allows God to speak through humans. Finally, speaking in tongues is a privately edifying phenomenon that should be practiced *before* teaching or preaching a sermon; it leads to greater clarity and purpose in public speaking and preaching. Some Christian communities today continue to think of glossolalia as a powerful, expansive, and indispensable spiritual practice that can encourage, advocate, heal, and spur the growth of church ministry.

1 Corinthians 15:1–58

Transformations: From "Psychic Body" to "Spiritual Body"

The Text in Its Ancient Context

Some have debated whether 1 Corinthians 15 belongs in this letter or is a segment of another writing with the theme of the resurrection. Most agree, however, that themes of the body, spirit, baptism, Christ's role, and the resurrection have been drawn from earlier in the letter and find their culmination in this, the final section of the body of the letter.

The chapter starts (vv. 1–11) with a defense and explanation of Paul's role in preaching the gospel, a role we know from Gal 1:11–2:10 was a matter of debate, even if the Acts of the Apostles solders into place Paul's authority in going to the gentiles (although not before giving Peter the primacy of place). Issues of Paul's identity and authority often surface in different ways in his letters—we need only to glance at the beginning of Galatians to see that he strongly defines his role as apostle with *no* connections to human authority there; in Romans, a community he does not know, he begins more cautiously with an unqualified self-designation as "apostle" and by describing himself more humbly as "slave of Christ." In 1 Cor. 15:1–11, Paul traces a proto-creedal statement that predates him (he uses a form of *paradidōmi*, a verb used to indicate the transmission of knowledge from a teacher, or by tradition, in his statement "what I in turn had received," 15:3) and links it to an authoritative line of transmission. Of "first importance" is that "Christ died for our sins in accordance with the scriptures, and that he was buried, and that he was raised on the third day in accordance with the scriptures" (vv. 3–4). Paul began his letter by emphasizing the crucifixion of Christ. Here, near the letter's end, he returns to the theme of Christ's death and elaborates on the theme of resurrection and the idea of death's overthrow.

Paul then traces the authoritative line of eyewitnesses, beginning with Cephas, then the Twelve, and the line continues "to all the apostles," then to James. Paul does not mention women in this list, though later sources would name Mary Magdalene and others. Paul states that he is "last of all": "as to one untimely born, [Christ] appeared also to me" (15:8). Paul locates his unfitness to be called an apostle *not* in the lack of ties he has to the historical Jesus or his lack of training in Jerusalem, but in his persecution of the *ekklēsia* of God. The proto-creedal statement recedes as Paul articulates that it does not matter whether it was "I or those" who preached and "so you believed," reprising the theme of various leaders at the beginning of his letter.

In verses 12 and following, Paul accuses the Corinthians of saying that "there is no resurrection of the dead" and argues the futility of this point of view (vv. 12–19) to those who are in Christ. We cannot know if the Corinthians actually claimed that there was no resurrection of the dead; indeed, this seems unlikely given that they baptize on behalf of the dead. Perhaps the Corinthians were emphasizing the power of resurrection in the present, even as they also emphasized Wisdom's power evidenced in their community through spiritual gifts. Paul then proceeds to defend the idea that Christ has been raised from the dead. He does so by turning to the story of creation and a typology that pairs Adam and Christ, with the first bringing death ("for as all die in Adam") and the second life ("so all will be made alive in Christ," v. 22).

Arguments from creation and arguments about Adam were commonplace at the time of Paul's writing of 1 Corinthians. Commentaries and philosophical debates over Plato's *Timaeus*, a story of the origins and structure of the cosmos, were penned; so, too, we find interpretations of Genesis that result in texts like the radical retelling of Genesis 1-2 in the *Hypostasis of the Archons* (perhaps second century CE). Jews contemporary with Paul engaged in debate over Genesis, sometimes with quite different interpretations, as we find in Philo's comment that all humans are a degeneration from the first human, who was "beautiful and good" and "lovely of body," compounded from the most pure and refined earthly substance (*Opif.* 137–40).

Portions of 1 Corinthians 15 remix 1 Thess. 4:13–5:11, with its eschatological themes. Here, as there, Paul offers an image of the Parousia or appearance of Christ in power (15:23). Paul employs language of the "reign of God" (15:24) and the destruction of "every ruler and authority and power." Given that the last of these to be destroyed is death, we can understand that, for the Corinthians hearing this letter, both temporal and cosmological rulers would be brought to mind, providing a coda to Paul's mention of "rulers of this age" crucifying "the Lord of glory" (2:8). Paul indicates that Christ's role should be understood in light of the Jewish Scriptures (Pss. 8:6; 110:1). Understanding this death-slaying Christ in relation to the psalmist's phrase "all things are put in subjection under his feet" might raise the question of whether he who subjected things is then superior or equal to God. Paul reassures the community that the Son is subject to God (15:28), dispelling any concerns or ideas that his theology involved "two powers in heaven," as did other, debated Jewish theologies of antiquity (Boyarin 2010; 2001).

Paul had begun this elaboration of the resurrection of the dead by stridently accusing the Corinthians of claiming there is no resurrection of the dead. He abruptly shifts back to them and to their practices, namely, baptism on behalf of the dead. This is the earliest and only reference in the Letters of Paul to such a practice, and it has raised many questions. The Corinthians may have been concerned about incorporating their ancestors into their new cult, and so baptism was a mechanism for initiating not only the living but also the dead (DeMaris). This practice becomes the grounds for Paul to insist on the truth of resurrection of the dead—not just of Christ but also of Christ as first evidence of a greater transformation.

In verse 35, Paul either paraphrases or caricatures a question from someone at Corinth: "How are the dead raised? With what kind of body do they come?" The answer is a full-scale blast in which Paul combines theories from religion and physics. Paul uses the metaphor of a kernel of grain, and argues that there are different kinds of flesh (*sarx*) and different kinds of bodies (*sōmata*), which themselves have different glories (*doxai*). We should think about this, as well as other aspects of 1 Corinthians, in light of scientific theories of the first century, a time when philosophical and theological speculation were often one and the same, and when theories from physics and medicine informed such speculation. For instance, while we may think of "spirit" as immaterial, Stoic philosophers of antiquity thought of it as a purer form of matter (Engberg-Pedersen).

This speculation from physics becomes the ground for further defining the "resurrection of the dead" and the particular problematic of the body. Paul lists a set of hierarchical binaries: weakness, power; physical, spiritual; first Adam, last Adam. Again, Paul argues from the creation story that the first Adam was a living soul, while the last Adam is a life-giving spirit. This language of *psychikon* versus *pneumatikon* echoes the hierarchical use of the terms in chapter 4 and may indicate some debate over the evolution or development of bodies from one kind of coarse matter to a finer kind of matter associated with spirit or *pneuma* (Engberg-Pedersen, 39–74). Certainly this language was quickly taken up and discussed by Paul's later interpreters. Origen tried to resolve the fact that Paul insisted the resurrected body was not flesh and blood, yet was a body (*De princ.* 2.10–11), while other early Christians, concerned about the continuation of the appetites after death, debated whether the resurrected body would have teeth or genitalia (Petrey).

Paul reprises and develops a vision of the end that he articulated in an earlier letter, 1 Thessalonians. This letter uses language of "putting on" (15:53) imperishability and immortality, imagery of clothing and unclothing, that probably called to mind baptismal practices (see 2 Cor. 5:1–5; Gal. 3:27).

The Text in the Interpretive Tradition

Paul's claim to have met Jesus "by revelation" (*apokalypsis* or cognates: Gal. 1:12, 16) and his lack of a familial or historical link to the earliest Jesus traditions or Jesus himself was a bone of contention among those in Christ in the first and second centuries and beyond. The Corinthians, among other communities, may have wanted to hear from an apostle who visited them a recital and confirmation of the "tradition" that Paul mentions in 1 Cor. 15:1–11; that is, they may have preferred someone who had known Jesus "in the flesh." Paul instead presents to them in writing "what I also received" (15:3) and explains how Christ appeared to him (15:6), using this revelation both to authorize his role as apostle and to present himself as called and chosen, echoing language of the Jewish prophets (Gal. 1:15)—not as a convert to a new religion (Stendahl).

This self-presentation would have many effects in the interpretive tradition. First, some would take up Paul's language of call, apocalypse, and visionary experience (see also 2 Cor. 12:1–13) and produce a text like the *Apocalypse of Paul*, found among the documents at Nag Hammadi, in which Paul is caught up into the heavens as he travels on his way to Jerusalem. Others, whose stance is represented in the Pseudo-Clementine literature (compiled in the fourth century CE but including sources that date to the second century CE), implicitly criticized Paul's claims as illegitimate, attributing to Jesus the saying that the "evil one" would also send apostles (*Clementine Hom.* 11.35.3). A fictional scene is set: The apostle Peter argues with "Simon"—a *magus*-figure whom Christians often evoked to represent their opponents—who is a lightly veiled stand-in for Paul. Peter challenges the truth of the sort of knowledge that comes through visionary experience, demonstrates that visions often occur to the impious rather than to the blessed, and finally spurts out: "So even if our Jesus did appear in a dream to you, making himself known and conversing with you, he did so in anger, speaking to an opponent. That is why he spoke to you through visions and dreams—through revelations which are external" (*Clementine Hom.* 17.19.1 [Meeks and Fitzgerald]). While it is clear that Paul's letters are very influential today, especially in

Protestant Christianity, ancient texts also indicate a strong ambivalence about Paul's letters, on the one hand—letters that were, after all, much interpreted among Christians who would come to be called heretics (followers of Valentinus, for instance) as well as those who would come to be considered orthodox (John Chrysostom, for example). In addition, some ancient texts show a strong skepticism regarding claims for revelation, questioning whether a visionary experience of Christ (like Paul's) could be false. Many of those who heard Paul's message in antiquity were more skeptical of it than most Christians, and those who use Paul's thought for political theology, are today. Those who understand Christ primarily through the lens of Paul (some do call themselves Paulinists!) or who would argue, with Slavoj Žižek, that "There is no Christ outside Saint Paul," miss early Christian controversy and even rejection of Paul and his letters. The versions of Christianity prevalent today, especially in North American Protestantism, make it hard to picture what a Christian identity that rejects Paul would look like, or even to engage in the work of historical reconstruction of the voices of the Corinthians or others who may have debated or rejected Paul's teachings in the first century.

The Text in Contemporary Discussion

Colossians 3:1–3, a pseudepigraphic text that claims to have been penned by Paul, offers the idea: "So if you have been raised with Christ, seek the things that are above, where Christ is . . . For you have died, and your life is hidden with Christ in God." As we have seen, some at Corinth may have understood themselves to have been living already, through the initiatory ritual of baptism, in a transformed, resurrected type of life. Colossians 3:1 takes up the themes of Paul's writings and transforms them more explicitly into the idea that Christians have already died and been raised with Christ, even in their present lives.

Karl Barth's 1924 *Die Auferstehung der Toten* decidedly rejects the idea that the resurrection occurs in the present: "It is not we who are the risen ones!" he exclaimed (Janssen, 65). Barth understood 1 Corinthians 15 as "the very peak and crown of this essentially critical and polemically negative Epistle" (Barth, 101) and "a clue to its meaning" (Barth, 5). It is a doctrine of last things, for Barth, which points to the gap between humans and God and the gap between now and then.

> Because it is *thus within* our existence, even our Christian existence, and must always be, however high we climb, because the "then" is really a *Then* and *There*, no Now and Here, the *reality* of the resurrection is exclusively the reality of the *resurrection*, the truth of Christianity is exclusively *God's* truth, its absoluteness is exclusively *God's* absoluteness. (Barth, 210–11)

In contrast, Rudolf Bultmann's appreciative 1926 response to Barth emphasizes that "our resurrection is reality, now that Christ is risen" (Janssen, 76). He explains: "in a certain sense, i.e. in so far as we belong to Christ, we are the resurrected, are the 'first fruits' . . . , are a 'new creation' " (Bultmann, 93–94). In this contrast between Barth and Bultmann we may see an echo of Paul's and some Corinthians' differing interpretations of the resurrection: Paul with Barth would insist on perfection or completion and resurrection as happening *then*, not now; think of his insistence, for example, in 1 Cor. 13:12: "For now we see in a mirror, dimly, but then we will see face to face." Some of the Corinthians, in contrast, may have delighted in spiritual gifts and in demonstrating the *now* of the new creation.

1 Corinthians 16:1–23
Epistolary Closing

The Text in Its Ancient Context

First Corinthians 15, with its crescendo of criticism of the Corinthians for their questions about the resurrection of the dead and compelling and varied arguments about the truth of the resurrection of the dead, its connection to the first and last Adam, and its ability literally to transform individuals and the cosmos, thundered at the end. Chapter 16, the closing of the letter, offers a quiet denouement and a glimpse of everyday life.

The letter first reminds its readers about the "contribution for the holy ones" (or "saints") and indicates that Paul has some expectation of equity among communities, since he has written the same to the *ekklēsiai* of Galatia. We also find, in 2 Corinthians 8 and 9, more letters about this contribution (see Georgi). We glimpse something of travel and social networks as Paul explains how to collect money and that he will send some emissary/ies, whom the Corinthians approve, with a letter—and funds—to Jerusalem.

Paul concludes with travel plans, as is typical of his letters, and reveals that he is likely in Ephesus as he writes. The social networks that Paul hints at or reveals earlier in the letter here arise again: the question of when Timothy and Apollos will visit Corinth is raised; the visit of Stephanas and Fortunatus and Achaicus to Paul, making up for the absence of the entire community, is mentioned, and their authority is enforced with the injunction to "be subject" to them and to "everyone who works and toils with them" (16:16). The epistle began with Paul's mention of Stephanas and "those in his household." The names Fortunatus and Achaicus hint at their servile or freedperson status, since one is nicknamed "fortunate," and the other is named after the region of his origin; we can wonder if they were Stephanas's slaves or freedpersons. Social networks are further highlighted as Paul offers greetings from *ekklēsiai* of Asia and mentions Aquila and Priscilla, whose names also appear in Romans 16.

Certain rituals and mechanics are exposed at the end of the letter. Perhaps like Romans—we know from Rom. 16:22 that the scribe Tertius wrote the letter—1 Corinthians was penned by a scribe, since Paul emphasizes his own writing at the end of the letter, probably in a note and signature, as was common in ancient letter writing.

The Text in the Interpretive Tradition

Paul ends 1 Corinthians by reprising his mention of Stephanas and household at the beginning of the letter and names them "the first converts in Achaia." This may have aided in the invention of 3

Corinthians. This text is known from the Armenian Bible and the commentary of Ephrem; it also seems to have circulated as part of a larger *Acts of Paul* (Schneemelcher, 217). Third Corinthians consists of a fragmentary letter purporting to be from Stephanas "and the presbyters (or ambassadors) who are with him," and Paul's reply. The Corinthians' letter to Paul expresses concern about the teachings of two men in Corinth who are introducing new ideas, such as that one should not appeal to the prophets, that there is no resurrection of the flesh, that Christ was not born of Mary nor came in the flesh, that the creation is not God's work. A brief narrative element before "Paul's" reply claims that Stephanas's letter was delivered to Paul in Philippi, where he was in prison, and he sent a reply to the theological confusion introduced by these false teachers.

From the fictive correspondence of 3 Corinthians we see the staying power of certain names, like Stephanas's, in what became the Christian tradition. We also learn more of the ancient context in which early Christians wrote letters in Paul's name and imaginatively responded to new social and theological crises in "Paul's" voice. Such responses in Paul's name, but not by Paul, include New Testament writings like Colossians, Ephesians, and the Pastoral Epistles (1 and 2 Timothy, Titus), as well as "letters" to and from Paul, like 3 Corinthians. The epistle was a powerful literary tool not only among early Christians. This phenomenon, called "epistolary narrative" or "epistolary fiction" (Rosenmeyer), burgeoned in antiquity; letters of Plato, Socrates, and others were invented to provide biographical details or to tease out the philosophical importance of famous figures. In using pseudepigraphical letters to create new narratives, early Christians were taking part in a larger cultural phenomenon that we need not understand as forgery or deception. Rather, Christians (among others) were in their writings creating possible worlds in which a figure like Paul, even after his death, was wielded to support Christian communities' responses to theological difference with "his" authoritative voice. These pseudepigraphical letters represent the multiple and even opposing directions in which Paul's teachings could be taken.

The Text in Contemporary Discussion

First Corinthians 16:2 discusses raising funds for a gift to be carried to Jerusalem: "On the first day of every week, each of you is to put aside and save whatever extra you earn, so that collections need not be taken when I come." The seeming conditional link between storing up money for the Jerusalem collection, on the one hand, and prosperity, on the other, makes the verse a possible source for those debating the "prosperity gospel."

Creflo Dollar, a famous pastor associated with the prosperity gospel, uses 1 Cor. 16:2, among other texts, to discuss the idea of prosperity in Bible study notes titled "The Secret Combination for True Prosperity" (Dollar). His Bible study notes argue that definitions of prosperity changed over time in biblical writings, and that 1 Cor. 16:2 is evidence of prosperity as "success in profitability and material gain." Although he reframes prosperity in terms of the total wholeness of the person, with money as only one aspect of prosperity, Dollar nonetheless reveals a larger debate going on among those who adhere to the prosperity gospel: which scriptural passages promise prosperity, and what do the same verses enjoin in terms of contributions (understood in contemporary churches as weekly tithes) that individuals may make?

This use of 1 Cor. 16:2 in the context of a broad range of biblical passages on "prosperity" reminds us, too, of how this strategy of interpretation is both fair use and misuse of Paul's letters. It is fair use because Paul's letters are indeed now part of a canon and as such can be juxtaposed with texts in a different language, from a different time period and context, in a creative theological way. But such a strategy is also misuse, because Paul's letters were in their first instantiation occasional, rather than works of systematic theology, to be picked over and juxtaposed with other "Scriptures." They were produced and received in an ad hoc, improvisational context by those who did not bear the name Christian, much less know that the letters would emerge into a canon of Pauline Letters or that some would put pen to papyrus to "imitate" Paul as he had enjoined (but perhaps not as he would have wished), writing letters in his name. The Letters of Paul were produced and received by those who could not imagine them embedded within a canon. It is our responsibility to pursue a letter like 1 Corinthians with a disciplined intimacy that calls us to see the text first as stranger, not at all written to us, or about us, and only later to see the text as intimate, as a fruitful interlocutor for the theological imagination, for political action, for religious practice today.

WORKS CITED

Agamben, Giorgio. 2005. *The Time That Remains: A Commentary on the Letter to the Romans*. Translated by Patricia Dailey. Stanford: Stanford University Press.

Ascough, Richard S., Philip A. Harland, and John S. Kloppenborg. 2012. *Associations in the Greco-Roman World: A Sourcebook*. Waco: Baylor University Press.

Ashton, John. 2000. *The Religion of Paul the Apostle*. New Haven: Yale University Press.

Badiou, Alain. 2003. *Saint Paul: The Foundation of Universalism*. Translated by Ray Brassier. Stanford: Stanford University Press.

Bagnall, Roger S., and Bruce W. Frier. 2006. *The Demography of Roman Egypt*. Cambridge: Cambridge University Press.

Bartchy, S. Scott. 1973. *Mallon Chrēsai: First Century Slavery and the Interpretation of 1 Corinthians 7:21*. Atlanta: Scholars Press.

Barth, Karl. 1933. *The Resurrection of the Dead*. Translated by H. J. Stenning. London: Hodder and Stoughton.

Baur, F. C. 1831. "Die Christuspartei in der korinthischen Gemeinde, der Gegensatz des petrinischen und paulinischen Christentums in der ältesten Kirche, der Apostel Petrus in Rom," *Tübinger Zeitschrift für Theologie* 4:61–206.

BeDuhn, Jason David. 1999. "Because of the Angels: Unveiling Paul's Anthropology in 1 Corinthians 11." *JBL* 118, no. 2:295–320.

Bishop, Rufus, and Seth Youngs Wells, eds. 1816. *Testimonies of the Life, Character, Revelation and Doctrines of Our Ever Blessed Mother Ann Lee*. Hancock, MA: J. Tallcott and J. Deming, Junrs.

Bookidis, Nancy, and Ronald S. Stroud. 1997. *Corinth XVIII, Part III: The Sanctuary of Demeter and Kore: Topography and Architecture*. Princeton: ASCSA.

Boyarin, Daniel. 2001. "The Gospel of the Memra: Jewish Binitarianism and the Prologue to John." *HTR* 94, no. 3:243–84.

Boyarin, Daniel. 2010. "Beyond Judaisms: Metatron and the Divine Polymorphy of Ancient Judaism." *Journal for the Study of Judaism* 41:323–365.

Buell, Denise Kimber. 2005. *Why This New Race: Ethnic Reasoning in Early Christianity*. New York: Columbia University Press.

Bultmann, Rudolf. 1987. *Faith and Understanding*. Vol. 1. Translated by Louise Pettibone Smith. Edited by Robert W. Funk. Minneapolis: Fortress Press.

Cadbury, Henry J. 1934. "The Macellum of Corinth." *JBL* 53, no. 2:134–41.

Calvin, John. 1981. *Commentary on the Epistles of Paul the Apostle to the Corinthians*. Translated by John Pringle. Grand Rapids: Baker.

Castelli, Elizabeth A. 1991. *Imitating Paul: A Discourse of Power*. Louisville: Westminster John Knox.

Clement of Alexandria. 1994. "The Stromata, or Miscellanies." In *ANF* 2:299–568.

Cohen, Shaye J. D. 1999. *The Beginnings of Jewishness: Boundaries, Varieties, Uncertainties*. Berkeley: University of California Press.

Concannon, Cavan. 2014. *"When You Were Gentiles": Specters of Ethnicity in Roman Corinth and Paul's Corinthian Correspondence*. New Haven: Yale University Press.

Conzelmann, Hans. 1975. *1 Corinthians: A Commentary on the First Epistle to the Corinthians*. Hermeneia. Philadelphia: Fortress Press.

"Decree on Ecumenism, *Unitatis redintegratio*." 1964. Documents of the II Vatican Council. http://www.vatican.va/archive/hist_councils/ii_vatican_council/documents/vat-ii_decree_19641121_unitatis-redintegratio_en.html.

Deissmann, Adolf. 1908. *Licht vom Osten: das Neue Testament und die neuentdeckten Texte der hellenistisch-römischen Welt*. Tübingen: Mohr.

DeMaris, Richard E. 1995. "Corinthian Religion and Baptism for the Dead (1 Corinthians 15:29): Insights from Archaeology and Anthropology." *JBL* 114, no. 4:661–82.

Dollar, Creflo. 2006. "The Secret Combination for True Prosperity." *Creflo Dollar Ministries*. http://www.creflodollarministries.org/BibleStudy/StudyNotes.aspx?id=62.

Douglas, Mary. 1970. *Natural Symbols*. London: Barrie & Rockliff.

Eisenbaum, Pamela. 2009. *Paul Was Not a Christian: The Original Message of a Misunderstood Apostle*. New York: HarperCollins.

Ekroth, Gunnel. 2007. "Meat in Ancient Greece: Sacrificial, Sacred or Secular?" *Food and History* 5:249–72.

Elliott, Neil. *Liberating Paul: The Justice of God and the Politics of the Apostle.* Maryknoll, NY: Orbis, 1994.

Engberg-Pedersen, Troels. 2010. *Cosmology and Self in the Apostle Paul: The Material Spirit.* New York: Oxford University Press.

Fee, Gordon D. 1987. *The First Epistle to the Corinthians.* NICNT. Grand Rapids: Eerdmans.

Fitzmyer, Joseph A. 2008. *First Corinthians: A New Translation with Introduction and Commentary.* AYB. New Haven: Yale University Press.

Frilingos, Christopher A. 2004. *Spectacles of Empire: Monsters, Martyrs, and the Book of Revelation.* Philadelphia: University of Pennsylvania Press.

Gaca, Kathy L. 2003. *The Making of Fornication: Eros, Ethics, and Political Reform in Greek Philosophy and Early Christianity.* Berkeley: University of California Press.

Gager, John G. 2000. *Reinventing Paul.* New York: Oxford University Press.

Garnsey, Peter, and Greg Woolf. 1989. "Patronage of the Rural Poor in the Roman World." In *Patronage in Ancient Society*, edited by Andrew Wallace-Hadrill, 153–70. London: Routledge.

Georgi, Dieter. 1992. *Remembering the Poor: The History of Paul's Collection for Jerusalem.* Nashville: Abingdon.

Glancy, Jennifer A. 2002. *Slavery in Early Christianity.* Oxford: Oxford University Press.

Gooch, Peter David. 1993. *Dangerous Food: I Corinthians 8–10 in Its Context.* Waterloo, ON: Wilfrid Laurier University Press.

Grabbe, Lester L. 1997. *Guide to the Apocrypha and Pseudepigrapha.* Vol. 3, *Wisdom of Solomon.* Sheffield: Sheffield Academic.

Haddad, Mimi. 2013. "Male Rule a Biblical Ideal? Part Two." *CBE International.* http://www.cbeinternational.org/?q=content/2013-09-12-male-rule-biblical-ideal-part-two-arise-e-newsletter.

Harrill, J. Albert. 1995. *The Manumission of Slaves in Early Christianity.* Tübingen: Mohr Siebeck.

Hodge, Caroline Johnson. 2007. *If Sons, Then Heirs: A Study of Kinship and Ethnicity in the Letters of Paul.* Oxford: Oxford University Press.

Horsley, Richard A. 1979. "Spiritual Marriage with Sophia." *VC* 33:30–54.

Horsley, Richard A. 1998. *1 Corinthians.* ANTC. Nashville: Abingdon.

Janssen, Claudia. 2000. "Bodily Resurrection (1 Cor. 15)? The Discussion of Resurrection in Karl Barth, Rudolf Bultmann, Dorothee Soelle and Contemporary Feminist Theology." *JSNT* 79:61–78.

Johnson-DeBaufre, Melanie. 2005. *Jesus among Her Children: Q, Eschatology, and the Construction of Christian Origins.* Cambridge, MA: Harvard University Press.

Johnson-DeBaufre, Melanie, and Laura S. Nasrallah. 2011. "Beyond the Heroic Paul: Toward a Feminist and Decolonizing Approach to the Letters of Paul." In *The Colonized Apostle: Paul Through Postcolonial Eyes*, edited by Christopher Stanley, 161–74. Minneapolis: Fortress Press.

Kampmann, Ursula. 1998. "Homonoia Politics in Asia Minor: The Example of Pergamon." In *Pergamon, Citadel of the Gods: Archaeological Record, Literary Description, and Religious Development*, edited by Helmut Koester, 373–93. Harrisburg, PA: Trinity Press International.

Kent, J. H. 1966. *Corinth VIII, Part III: The Inscriptions, 1926–1950*. Princeton: ASCSA.

King, Karen L. 2005. *What Is Gnosticism*? Cambridge, MA: Harvard University Press.

King, Martin Luther, Jr. 1956. "Paul's Letter to American Christians." *The King Center*. http://www.thekingcenter.org/archive/document/pauls-letter-american-christians-0.

Kloppenborg, John. 2013. "Membership Practices in Pauline Christ Groups." *Early Christianity* 4, no. 2:183–215.

Kocar, Alexander. 2013. "'Humanity Came to Be According to Three Essential Types': Ethical Responsibility and Practice in the Valentinian Anthropogony of the Tripartite Tractate (NHC I, 5)." In *Jewish and Christian Cosmogony in Late Antiquity*, edited by Lance Jenott and Sarit Kattan Gribetz, 193–221. Tübingen: Mohr Siebeck.

Koester, Helmut. 1990. *Ancient Christian Gospels: Their History and Development*. Harrisburg, PA: Trinity Press International.

Kovacs, Judith L. 2005. *1 Corinthians: Interpreted by Early Christian Medieval Commentators*. The Church's Bible. Grand Rapids: Eerdmans.

Lamp, Jeffrey S. 2000. *First Corinthians 1–4 in Light of Jewish Wisdom Traditions: Christ, Wisdom, and Spirituality*. Lewiston, NY: Mellen.

Lieu, Judith. 2002. *Neither Jew Nor Greek? Constructing Early Christianity*. London: T&T Clark.

Luther, Martin. 1973. *LW* 28.

Marchal, Joseph A. 2011. "The Usefulness of an Onesimus: The Sexual Use of Slaves and Paul's Letter to Philemon." *JBL* 130, no. 4:749–70.

Martin, Dale B. 1990. *Slavery as Salvation: The Metaphor of Slavery in Pauline Christianity*. New Haven: Yale University Press.

Martin, Dale B. 1995. *The Corinthian Body*. New Haven: Yale University Press.

Martin, Dale B. 2006. *Sex and the Single Savior*. Louisville: Westminster John Knox.

Meeks, Wayne A. 2003. *The First Urban Christians: The Social World of the Apostle Paul*. 2nd ed. New Haven: Yale University Press.

Meeks, Wayne A., and John T. Fitzgerald. 2007. *The Writings of St. Paul: Annotated Texts, Reception and Criticism*. New York: Norton.

Meggitt, Justin J. 1998. *Paul, Poverty, and Survival*. Edinburgh: T&T Clark.

Miller, Anna C. 2013. "*Not with Eloquent Wisdom*: Democratic *Ekklēsia* Discourse in 1 Corinthians 1–4." *JSNT* 35:323–54.

Miller, Donald E., and Tetsunao Yamamori. 2007. *Global Pentecostalism: The New Face of Christian Social Engagement*. Berkeley: University of California Press.

Millis, Benjamin W. 2010. "The Social and Ethnic Origins of the Colonists in Early Roman Corinth." In *Corinth in Context: Comparative Studies on Religion and Society*, edited by Steven J. Friesen, Daniel N. Schowalter, and James C. Walters, 13–36. Leiden: Brill.

Millis, Benjamin W. 2013. "The Local Magistrates and Elite of Roman Corinth." In *Corinth in Contrast: Studies in Inequality*, edited by Steven J. Friesen, Sarah A. James, and Daniel N. Schowalter, 38–53. Leiden: Brill.

Mitchell, Margaret M. 1991. *Paul and the Rhetoric of Reconciliation: An Exegetical Investigation of the Language and Composition of 1 Corinthians*. Tübingen: Mohr Siebeck.

Mitchell, Margaret M. 2002. *The Heavenly Trumpet: John Chrysostom and the Art of Pauline Interpretation*. Louisville: Westminster John Knox.

Morin, France. 2001. *Heavenly Visions: Shaker Gift Drawings and Gift Songs*. Minneapolis: University of Minnesota Press.

Mount, Christopher. 2005. "1 Corinthians 11:3–16: Spirit Possession and Authority in a Non-Pauline Interpolation." *JBL* 124, no. 2:313–40.

Mouritsen, Henrik. 2011. *The Freedman in the Roman World*. Cambridge: Cambridge University Press.

Musurillo, Herbert, trans. 1972. *The Acts of the Christian Martyrs*. Oxford: Clarendon Press.

Myung, Sung-hoon, and Yonggi Hong, eds. 2003. *Charis and Charisma: David Yonggi Cho and the Growth of Yoido Full Gospel Church*. Oxford: Regnum.

Nabers, Ned Parker. 1967. *Macella: A Study in Roman Archaeology*. Princeton: Princeton University Press.

Naiden, F. S. 2013. *Smoke Signals for the Gods: Ancient Greek Sacrifice from the Archaic through Roman Periods*. New York: Oxford University Press.

Nasrallah, Laura Salah. 2004. *An Ecstasy of Folly: Prophecy and Authority in Early Christianity*. Cambridge, MA: Harvard University Press.

Nasrallah, Laura Salah. 2012. "Grief in Corinth: The Roman City and Paul's Corinthian Correspondence." In *Contested Spaces: Houses and Temples in Roman Antiquity and the New Testament*, edited by David L. Balch and Annette Weissenrieder, 109–40. Tübingen: Mohr Siebeck.

Nasrallah, Laura Salah. 2013. "'You Were Bought with a Price': Freedpersons and Things in 1 Corinthians." In *Corinth in Contrast: Studies in Inequality*, edited by Steven J. Friesen, Sarah A. James, and Daniel N. Schowalter, 54–73. Leiden: Brill.

Nasrallah, Laura Salah. 2014. "Archaeology and the Pauline Letters." In *Oxford Handbook of Pauline Studies*, edited by Barry Matlock. New York: Oxford University Press.

Neyrey, Jerome. 1986. "Body Language in 1 Corinthians: The Use of Anthropological Models for Understanding Paul and His Opponents." *Semeia* 35:129–70.

Økland, Jorunn. 2010. "Ceres, Κόρη, and Cultural Complexity: Divine Personality Definitions and Human Worshippers in Roman Corinth." In *Corinth in Context: Comparative Studies on Religion and Society*, edited by Steven J. Friesen, Daniel N. Schowalter, and James C. Walters, 199–229. Leiden: Brill.

Oldfather, W. A., trans. 1925. *Epictetus: Discourses, Books 1–2*. LCL 131. Cambridge, MA: Harvard University Press.

Oster, Richard. 1988. "When Men Wore Veils to Worship: the Historical Context of 1 Corinthians 11.4." *NTS* 34, no. 4:481–505.

Pétrement, Simone. 1990. *A Separate God: the Christian Origins of Gnosticism*. Translated by Carol Harrison. San Francisco: HarperSanFrancisco.

Petrey, Taylor. 2010. "Carnal Resurrection: Sexuality and Sexual Difference in Early Christianity." ThD diss., Harvard University Divinity School.

Pervo, Richard I. 2008. *Acts: A Commentary*. Hermeneia. Minneapolis: Fortress Press.

Price, S. R. F. 1985. *Rituals and Power: The Roman Imperial Cult in Asia Minor*. Cambridge: Cambridge University Press.

Robinson, Elizabeth A. 2011. *Histories of Peirene: A Corinthian Fountain in Three Millennia*. Princeton: ASCSA.

Rosenmeyer, Patricia A. 2001. *Ancient Epistolary Fictions: the Letter in Greek Literature*. Cambridge: Cambridge University Press.

Ruyt, Claire de. 1983. *Macellum, marché alimentaire des romains*. Louvain-la-Neuve: Institut supérieur d'archéologie et d'histoire de l'art, College Érasme.

Schmithals, Walter. 1971. *Gnosticism in Corinth: An Investigation of the Letters to the Corinthians*. Nashville: Abingdon.

Schneemelcher, Wilhelm, ed. 1992. *New Testament Apocrypha*. Vol. 2, *Writings Relating to the Apostles, Apocalypses and Related Subjects*. Rev. ed. Cambridge: James Clarke & Co.

Schüssler Fiorenza, Elisabeth. 1983. *In Memory of Her: A Feminist Theological Reconstruction of Christian Origins*. New York: Crossroad.

Schüssler Fiorenza, Elisabeth. 1987. "Rhetorical Situation and Historical Reconstruction in 1 Corinthians." *NTS* 33:386–403.

Schüssler Fiorenza, Elisabeth. 1993. *Discipleship of Equals: A Critical Feminist Ekklesia-logy of Liberation*. New York: Crossroad.

Schüssler Fiorenza, Elisabeth. 1994. *Jesus: Miriam's Child, Sophia's Prophet: Critical Issues in Feminist Christology*. New York: Continuum.

Schüssler Fiorenza, Elisabeth. 1999. *Rhetoric and Ethic: The Politics of Biblical Studies*. Minneapolis: Fortress Press.

Schweitzer, Albert. 1931. *The Mysticism of Paul the Apostle*. Translated by William Montgomery. New York: Henry Holt.

Shaner, Katherine. 2012. "Religion and the Civic Life of the Enslaved: A Case Study in Roman Ephesos." ThD Dissertation, Harvard University Divinity School.

Shewring, W. H., trans. 1929. *The Passion of Perpetua and Felicity*. London: The Fleuron. Modernized translation by Paul Halsall. 1996. "Medieval Sourcebook: St. Perpetua: *The Passion of Saints Perpetua and Felicity* 203." Internet Medieval Source Book. Fordham University Center for Medieval Studies. http://www.fordham.edu/halsall/source/perpetua.asp.

Skogen, Dan. 2009. "The Battle Continues For Nebraska Church Formerly Affiliated With the ELCA." *Exposing the ELCA*. http://www.exposingtheelca.com/exposed-blog/the-battle-continues-for-nebraska-church-formerly-affiliated-with-the-elca.

Slane, Kathleen Warner. 2000. "East-West Trade in Fine Wares and Commodities: the View from Corinth." *RCRFActa* 36:299–312.

Smith, James K. A. 2010. *Thinking in Tongues: Pentecostal Contributions to Christian Philosophy*. Grand Rapids: Eerdmans.

Smith, Jonathan Z. 2004. "Re: Corinthians." In *Relating Religion: Essays in the Study of Religion*, 340–61. Chicago: University of Chicago Press.

Spawforth, A. J. S. 1996. "Roman Corinth: The Formation of a Colonial Elite." In *Roman Onomastics in the Greek East: Social and Political Aspects*, edited by A. D. Rizakis, 167–82. Paris: Diffusion de Boccard.

Stang, Charles M. 2012. *Apophasis and Pseudonymity in Dionysius the Areopagite: "No Longer I."* New York: Oxford University Press.

Stendahl, Krister. 1976. *Paul Among Jews and Gentiles and Other Essays*. Minneapolis: Fortress Press.

Sterling, Gregory E. 1995. "Wisdom among the Perfect: Creation Traditions in Alexandrian Judaism and Corinthian Christianity." *NovT* 37, no. 4:355–84.

Still, E. Coye, III. 2002. "The Meaning and Uses of *EIDOLOTHYTON* in First Century Non-Pauline Literature and 1 Cor 8:1–11:1: Toward Resolution of the Debate." *Trinity Journal* 23, no. 2:225–34.

Stowers, Stanley K. 2011a. "Kinds of Myth, Meals, and Power: Paul and the Corinthians." In *Redescribing Paul and the Corinthians*, edited by Ron Cameron and Merrill P. Miller, 105–50. Atlanta: Society of Biblical Literature.

Stowers, Stanley K. 2011b. "Does Pauline Christianity Resemble a Hellenistic Philosophy?" In *Redescribing Paul and the Corinthians*, edited by Ron Cameron and Merrill P. Miller, 219–44. Atlanta: Society of Biblical Literature.

Stowers, Stanley K. 2011c. "The Concept of 'Community' and the History of Early Christianity." *Method and Theory in the Study of Religion* 23, nos. 3–4:238–56.

Svebakken, Hans. 2012. *Philo of Alexandria's Exposition of the Tenth Commandment*. Atlanta: Society of Biblical Literature.

Theissen, Gerd. 1982. *The Social Setting of Pauline Christianity: Essays on Corinth*. Edited and translated by John H. Schütz. Philadelphia: Fortress Press.

Thiselton, Anthony C. 2000. *The First Epistle to the Corinthians*. NIGTC. Grand Rapids: Eerdmans.

United Society of Believers, Commonly Called Shakers. 1848. "A Summary View of the Millennial Church." *Pass the Word Services*. http://www.passtheword.org/shaker-manuscripts/Millennial-Church/mchrch4x.htm.

Weissenrieder, Annette. 2012. "'Do You Not Know That You Are God's Temple?' Towards a New Perspective on Paul's Temple Image in 1 Corinthians 3:16." In *Contested Spaces: Houses and Temples in Roman Antiquity and the New Testament*, edited by David L. Balch and Annette Weissenrieder, 377–412. Tübingen: Mohr Siebeck.

West, A. B. 1931. *Corinth VIII, Part II: Latin Inscriptions, 1896–1926*. Cambridge, MA: ASCSA.

Wilckens, Ulrich. 1959. *Weisheit und Torheit: Eine exegetisch-religionsgeschichtliche Untersuchung zu 1 Kor 1 und 2*. *BHTh*, 26. Tübingen: Mohr.

Williams, Charles K., II. 1993. "Roman Corinth as a Commercial Center." In *The Corinthia in the Roman Period (JRASup 8)*, edited by T. E. Gregory, 31–46. Ann Arbor: JRA.

Winter, Bruce W. 2001. *After Paul Left Corinth: The Influence of Secular Ethics and Social Change*. Grand Rapids: Eerdmans.

Wire, Antoinette Clark. 1990. *The Corinthian Women Prophets: A Reconstruction through Paul's Rhetoric.* Minneapolis: Fortress Press.

World Council of Churches. 2014. "Week of Prayer for Christian Unity." World Council of Churches. http://www.oikoumene.org/en/press-centre/events/week-of-prayer-for-christian-unity.

Žižek, Slavoj. 2000. *The Fragile Absolute: or, Why is the Christian Legacy Worth Fighting For*? London: Verso.

2 Corinthians

David E. Fredrickson

Introduction

SECOND CORINTHIANS HAS impressed itself on scholars as a collection of originally separate Pauline writings, a quilt made of several letter fragments. The integrity of the letter has so been put in doubt that even Paul's authorship in the case of one passage (6:14–7:1) has, for plausible reasons, been called into question. The letter as we read it today appears to have seams, to have been sown together at a time unknown by an editor unnamed. Note the abrupt and, by current standards, inexplicable transitions between 2:13 and 14; 6:13 and 14; 7:1 and 2; 7:16 and 8:1; 8:24 and 9:1; and 9:15 and 10:1. For many interpreters, these appear to be awkwardly stitched together texts hinting at a history of compilation. And so it is frequently said that 2 Corinthians lacks argumentative flow. The simplest explanation is that the letter never possessed rhetorical unity since it was not in the strict sense *a* letter penned by Paul. This is the dominant scholarly opinion today, and it renders naïve any questions about the meaning of the letter considered as a whole, either in the first century, in the history of interpretation, or for modern readers.

Yet there is another way of reading 2 Corinthians, one that is not alarmed when letters written in or near the first century shift from topic to topic or change tone without warning (for the "mixed" type of letter, see Malherbe 1988, 73, 81). This approach bolsters the case for integrity by highlighting the continuity of themes and key terms across the letter. Along these lines, we might observe that the contrast Paul draws between himself and his opponents over severity and gentleness in leadership style runs throughout the letter, from 1:12 to 13:10 to be precise. Most importantly, this alternative way of reading defers final judgment concerning the letter's unity until it reconstructs events and emotions between Paul's sending of 1 Corinthians and his composition of 2 Corinthians. This present approach *presumes* the letter's unity and uses passages throughout to imagine a complicated situation between Paul and the church at Corinth, which only a complex letter, appearing to some readers as having seams, could even hope to address.

It appears, then, that we have arrived at a method of reading the letter. First, there is a need to discern the situation and then observe what Paul has to say to it. But a word of warning is in order: not only must our reconstruction remain tentative and open to revision, but we must also admit that the story of Paul and the Corinthians is entirely a Pauline fiction. (Actually, it is my fiction about Paul's fiction.) That is, there is no way for us to see through the letter to "what really happened" between the two Corinthian letters. All we have is the way *Paul* wants his readers to see what happened and what it all means. A clear division between context and text or between occasion and rhetoric is therefore an illusion. Paul's construal of persons, events, and emotions is rhetorical from the very start. That does not make the backstory of 2 Corinthians narrated below any less interesting. It does demand, however, that any interpretation, and that certainly includes this essay, confess that it is a fiction, provisional, and risks being taken in unanticipated directions. I emphasize this demand at the beginning of the essay, since habits of the biblical commentary genre will induce me to write as if I had forgotten it.

So where to begin in *imagining* the events and emotions as Paul wants his first readers to think of them? Second Corinthians 1:8–9 tells a dismal tale of Paul's journey in Asia, one of melancholy and thoughts of suicide. Christian writers of the fourth century, perhaps alarmed at the sadness of the apostle, thought Paul was describing external events: his arrest, a court's death sentence, and the apprehension anyone would feel in such circumstances (see Fredrickson 2000). But the phrase "we ourselves in ourselves had the sentence of death" (here and below, my own translation) would more likely have been understood in the first century as self-condemnation, the feelings that overwhelm the soul with regret or remorse. Regret arose from the paradox of the stern judge and convicted offender inhabiting the same body.

What did Paul have to regret? In 2 Cor. 7:8, he speaks plainly about the matter: he had written a letter to the church powerful enough to induce pain in the readers. He refers to this letter in 2:3–4 as he denies that it was his intention to cause grief, thus, of course, reinforcing our sense that he did. This is the so-called letter of tears, which has puzzled interpreters for centuries. John Chrysostom thought this letter was 1 Corinthians itself. Today some scholars identify it as 2 Corinthians 10–13, although a third opinion, one the present essayist shares, holds that the letter is lost and not to be identified with any extant Pauline writing and therefore a bit of a mystery (see Furnish, 163–68). But thanks to Ps.-Libanius and Ps.-Demetrius, unknown authors of the two surviving ancient epistolary handbooks, there are some helpful clues (see Malherbe 1988, 30–41, 66–81). These handbooks gave instructions on how to write a grieving letter (*epistolē lypētikē*), and when the many actual letters of grief in antiquity (e.g., Ps.-Demosthenes, *Ep.* 2) are also consulted, we learn that a letter writer's grieving self-presentation was intended, and understood by recipients, as stinging moral reproof (see Fredrickson 2001). To paraphrase the critical portion of these letters: "The tears through which I write are evidence of the grief your behavior has caused me."

What did the church at Corinth do to cause Paul pain? Paul hints in 2:1 at an unplanned visit to Corinth. He made this trip presumably because 1 Corinthians, the letter carried by Timothy, did not have its desired effect of discouraging the elite from displaying their social status, the main problem addressed in that letter. During this impromptu visit, Paul was injured or treated unjustly by some member of the church (Barrett 1970). He alludes to this event tactfully in 2:5 and mentions the offender directly in 7:12 ("the one who injured"), though still without naming him. He refers to himself as "the one injured." Here is the point: the church, for its part, took no action against the one who had treated Paul unjustly during his unplanned visit. So Paul fled to Ephesus and from a distance wrote the "letter of tears," rebuking the community for its indifference to the injury he suffered. Titus took this epistle to Corinth.

As Paul tells this story, when the letter arrived in Corinth under Titus's care it had a double effect. On the one hand, it caused the

Corinthian church grief, yes, but a "grief according to God," as Paul assures his readers, since the letter's severity issued in their repentance. That is, it aroused the readers' zeal for Paul (7:7, 11–12). On the other hand, the community's newfound resolve to discipline the offender was excessive; note the term "vengeance" (*ekdikēsis*) in 7:11. In its response to the letter of tears, then, it seems that the church swung around wildly from its former indifference to the offense committed against Paul. The harshness of their treatment of the offender is indicated in the term *epitimia*, which stands behind the English term "punishment" in 2:6. *Epitimia* held a special place in Greco-Roman moral exhortation. It was moral chastisement intended to cause shame, a particularly extreme measure in the honor-seeking society of the first century, especially if it was delivered in public (see Malherbe 1983). It was a commonplace worry for ancient moral guides in antiquity, except among harsh Cynics (see Malherbe 1989), that public reproof, particularly of young men, might result in suicide (see, e.g., Plutarch, *How to Tell a Flatterer from a Friend* 70F–71C). It is no wonder, then, that Paul expresses concern for the offender; he is liable to being "drunk down by excessive grief" (2:7), a euphemism for suicide.

The letter of tears had one more effect, though if we are to understand it, one more set of players in Corinth must be introduced. As if the relationship between Paul and the church were not complicated enough, missionaries critical of Paul's manner of ministry entered Corinth, most likely after his flight to Ephesus. In his absence, they competed with him (and with one another? see 2 Cor. 10:12) for the community's allegiance. Paul calls them "super-apostles" (2 Cor. 11:5 and 12:11) and characterizes them in terms reminiscent of harsh Cynic philosophers who sought to dominate those they led (Malherbe 1970). Again, it must be emphasized that this depiction of his rivals is Paul's: his portrayal of them as severe moralists accentuates his own image as conciliatory, gentle, and gracious. Yet the issue of Paul's free speech was far broader than Paul and his relationship with the Corinthians. A fundamental disagreement about the nature of frank speech raged (sometimes within the same author) from the Hellenistic period well into late antiquity:

Was it to be viewed as the verbal expression of the wise man's moral independence, or was it to be regarded as a means to improve others in the context of friendly relations? (For a study in *parrēsia* as display of freedom and as the art of moral improvement, see John Chrysostom's encomium of Babylas, *De sancto hieromartyre Babyla* [PG 50:541–46]).

What did these rival apostles think of the letter of tears? They praised it for its severity; but they also contrasted the letter's power at a distance with Paul's deficient physical presence and his ironic and deceptive spoken words. In what might be regarded as the earliest commentary on the Pauline Epistles, 2 Cor. 10:9–10 describes the characterization of Paul's own letters that he attributes to his rivals. The passage is saturated with terminology from ancient rhetorical handbooks and treatises. "To frighten," "weighty," and "strong" are the markers of "forcefulness" (*deinotēs*), a style of speaking in which orators, most notably in the ancient world Demosthenes (see Dionysius of Halicarnassus, *Demosthenes* 22), overwhelmed audiences. Two additional phrases indicate the super-apostles' familiarity with ancient rhetorical and literary criticism: "presence of the body" and "attenuated speech" (*ho logos exouthenēmenos*, my translation: see Fredrickson 2001). "They say" Paul's physical presence, a reference in rhetorical terms to oratorical delivery, is weak, and that he intentionally makes his speech less forceful than he could (as judged by the letters) and more like the utterings of persons of low esteem, much in the style of Socrates, whose ironic self-depreciation pricked holes in puffed-up dialogue partners. So the letter of tears was just one more piece of evidence that Paul in the church's presence was deceptive and lacked the frank speech, the quality of *deinotēs*, that marked true apostles. This charge of disparity between words and deeds Paul vigorously disputes in 10:10 and throughout the letter, as we will see below.

So here are the issues facing Paul on the eve of 2 Corinthians. First, Paul is in an impossible position. He must assert that he possesses frank speech, but the medium for his apology is a letter, and as he writes from a distance, he runs the risk of convicting himself of the very charges summarized in 10:9–10. This problem he takes up in 2 Cor. 2:14–4:6.

Second, the individual who wronged Paul has been isolated from the community; Paul exhorts the community to bring him back in 2:5–11. Third, even though the church responded to the letter of tears positively by disciplining the offender, the grief (or was it resentment or vexation?) lingered on; Paul confronts this issue in 4:7–7:16 as he places his frank speech into the ancient tradition of friendship, stresses his love for the church, and appeals for reconciliation. To further assuage hard feelings, he accentuates his regret for ever having written the letter (1:8–9 and 7:8). The final purpose of 2 Corinthians, if the present reconstruction of the letter's occasion is at all plausible, is to dissuade the church from recognizing the legitimacy of the super-apostles and their harsh form of leadership; this he does sporadically in 2 Corinthians 1–7 and pointedly in chapters 10–13.

Nothing has yet been said about 2 Corinthians 8–9. These chapters deal with the collection for the saints in Jerusalem. In 1 Cor. 16:1–9, Paul had tailored his travel plans around his pivotal role in organizing a fund from the churches of Galatia, Macedonia, and Corinth for the relief of communities in Jerusalem. The problem for Paul was how to encourage the Corinthians to make good on their promise to contribute without reinforcing the patron-client ideology that permeated all charitable activities in the Roman period. Gift-giving in general symbolized the social difference between giver and recipient and announced the former's power and superiority while emphasizing the latter's neediness and obligation to repay the gift through public glorification of the giver. This is precisely the problem Paul attacks so energetically in 1 Corinthians. It also explains why Paul shuns the financial support of the Corinthian elite in 2 Corinthians 10–13: simply put, he doesn't want to be owned (see Marshall). Finally, it is worth considering that domination hidden in the gift-giving of ancient society and potentially, Paul fears, in the collection for the saints in Jerusalem resembles the sovereignty in disciplinary matters that the super-apostles exhibit. In other words, patronal power and super-apostle severity are two instances of domination. Paul's opposition to any form of lordship that is not inhabited by the crucified Messiah is a central feature in all of his letters and especially here in 2 Corinthians. This makes him a sharp, if indirect, critic of empire.

2 Corinthians 1:1–7

The Sound of P

The Text in Its Ancient Context

The Greek letter *pi* (*p*) is repeated twenty-six times in these verses. There is comfort in the repetition of sounds, as in the sincere utterance of "there, there." Each time the letter *pi* is pronounced, lips meet, puffing a bit of breath toward the other person. An intimacy adheres to these hesitant vocalizations, a gentle insistence of breath. *Parakalō* and its noun cognate *paraklēsis* together occur ten times. Perhaps Paul entreats, or does he exhort? *Parakalō* could mean either, and it is impossible to say with certainty which is meant here. Another word starting with *pi* in this passage is *pathēma*. This word bears a double character also: it meant suffering, but included both exterior and interior aspects. Thus it signifies pain inflicted on Paul from without (beatings or maltreatment, for example), or it could refer to emotions themselves, like love, or regret (cf. Rom. 8:18; Phil. 3:10). It, with its cognate *paschein* ("to suffer"), occurs four times.

Paul clearly departed from his usual practice of beginning a letter by thanking God for the very issues he addresses in the rest of the text (e.g., 1 Cor. 1:4–9; Phil. 1:3–11). Does this mean that 1:3–7 is unrelated to the rest of the letter? Not at all. *Parakalō* ("I exhort" or "entreat") in its second sense anticipates the grace, gentleness, and forgiveness in Paul's manner of leadership in contrast to the severity of the super-apostles. Yet the dueling meaning within the one word also anticipates the movement of Paul between the reproof of the letter of tears and his begging for reconciliation.

Note further that in 1:3 Paul links his manner of ministry to divine names: the father of compassionate feelings (*oiktirmos* suggests the vocalizations of ritual lament, "keening" in other words) and the God of all exhorting/entreating. The association of Paul's grace in ministry with God's grace is the primary form of Paul's apology through the letter (e.g., 5:18–6:2). Similarly, in 1:5, Paul and Christ are, insofar as emotions (*pathēmata*) are concerned, indistinguishable (cf. Phil. 1:8), and that goes a long way to defending his form of ministry. Paul develops the motif of his sharing of emotions/suffering with Christ throughout the letter and includes the Corinthians in 1:6–7. Finally, in verse 7, he states his hope about the community; this is yet another way of exhorting/begging. The content of his hope (there is, incidentally, another *pi* in the middle of *elpis*) is unstated at this point, but the position of *paraklēsis* at the end of the sentence suggests the church has its own comforting to do by restoring the offender (2:7) and continuing to mend fences with Paul (1:13–14; 4:14–15; 6:20–7:4).

The Text in the Interpretive Tradition

Early Christian commentators took from these first verses clues to the nature of the whole letter and emphasized the "consolation" in the midst of suffering that Paul proclaims. Pelagius, however, focused on Paul's setting his name before his recipients, adopting "the custom of secular judges," because "he is an apostle who is writing to those who are accountable to him"; he thus emphasized the element of correction throughout the letter (*Commentary*).

It is also the case that commentators diminished the passionate side of many Pauline terms in this letter (e.g., see below on "weakness" in 13:4). Their treatment of *pathēmata* in 1:1–7 is no exception. I translated the word above as "emotions." The English "sufferings" expresses the view of early commentators that Paul has in mind things done to him, shipwreck or imprisonment for example, not stirrings within his soul difficult or impossible to control like grief or desire (see John Chrysostom, *In epistulam ii ad Corinthios* [*homiliae 1–30*, PG 61:579]; but for a combination of the inner and outer aspects see Theodorus Studites, *Epistulae* 252.15). A similar downplaying of passion can be seen in the case of *oiktirmos* (1:3). In the interpretive tradition, the word came to be defined by the benefactor and his *philanthropia* ("love for humanity"). This redefinition dulled the sharp edge of violent emotion conveyed by the word in the case, for example, of the widow or childless mother keening the death of her loved one (see John Chrysostom, *De corruptoribus virginum* [PG 60:744]). The New Testament itself is partly responsible for adding a sense of condescension to this term (see Luke 6:36), but beginning with Clement of Alexandria (*Protrepticus* 1.8.4), the Christian tradition substituted a philanthropic wish on God's part to save humanity and show it mercy for a divine desire for communion with humanity.

The Text in Contemporary Discussion

The "Father of all compassionate feelings and the God of all entreaties" (2 Cor. 1:3) is a weak and unsuitable God for those who, like the super-apostles, see church leadership in terms of issuing divine commands from a position of dispassionate invulnerability. The adequacy of the philosophical idea of impassibility for the representation of God in the Old Testament has been called into question by biblical interpreters (see, e.g., Fretheim). Christian theology's comfort with a self-constituting and self-sufficient God has been sharply critiqued by Jürgen Moltmann (1974) as he put a question to the tradition seldom asked in Christian theology: What did the death of the Son mean for the Father?

2 Corinthians 1:8–13

Reconciliation as Resurrection

The Text in Its Ancient Context

As previously noted, in 1:8–9 Paul uses the ancient rhetoric of regret to communicate to the church his turbulent emotional state after he sent the letter of tears but before he met up with Titus in Macedonia. Such self-disclosure might have itself been seen as a gesture of reconciliation (see Aristotle, *Nicomachean Ethics* 1110b 18–30), since Paul implies that he did not delight in criticizing the church. In fact, the uncertainty of his relationship with the community after he wrote severely weighs Paul down to the point of considering suicide, if his readers are to believe these self-revelations, as he makes his way through Asia.

Unlike those whose confidence is based on themselves (perhaps a dig at the super-apostles; see 3:5 and Phil. 3:2–4), Paul's boldness for life and ministry resides in his relationship to the church (see 1:14; cf. Phil. 4:1; 1 Thess. 2:19–20). For this reason, his report of rescue by the God who raises the dead is a theological interpretation of the Corinthians' change of heart reported by Titus (see 7:6–7). The church's (tentative?) steps toward Paul are portrayed as the working of God (cf. Phil 2:13), and in verses 10–11 he hopes for further rescue/reconciliation. Finally, it is significant that, located between two theologically rich understandings of the church as communion (1:11 and 14), we find the charge of "fleshly wisdom" leveled at Paul by the super-apostles. What Paul understands as a ministry growing out of the bonds of friendship, whose speech embodies "openness" and "sincerity" (both synonyms for *parrēsia*) and exhibits "the grace of God," his opponents characterize as rhetorical trickery. That fundamental tension between Paul and his rivals runs through 2 Corinthians from beginning to end.

The Text in the Interpretive Tradition

Early Christian commentators took Paul at his word when he declares his sincerity (*eilikrineia*), a term that in conjunction with *haplotēs* ("frankness," NRSV) in rhetorical theory was a matter of straightforward and clear language in contrast to artificiality and the concealment of figured speech (see Smiley, 219–24). John Chrysostom praised Paul for this very reason (*Homilies in 2 Cor.* [PG 61:405–6]). Theodoret of Cyrus was likewise impressed: Paul "teaches only what he has been taught by the grace of God, adding nothing of his own to it. . . . The facts speak for themselves and prove that he is right" (*Commentary*). The fathers' enthusiasm for Paul's *eilikrineia* may have come from the central role this term played in ancient rhetorical handbooks, where it connoted the opposite of irony, flattery, and particularly the moral criticism carried out under cover of rhetorical figures (Fiore). In short, early interpreters thought Paul's sincerity was synonymous with his *parrēsia*.

The Text in Contemporary Discussion

One dramatic difference between early Christian commentary on Paul's letters and contemporary scholarship is the attention given in the latter to Paul's persuasive speech, that is, rhetoric. Rather than presuming, for example, that Paul really has despaired of life and seeking to identify the "affliction" he suffered (1:8), scholars ask about the rhetorical effect of such claims. While this approach has proven very fruitful, and is employed in this essay, it sometimes raises the question of whether Paul was manipulative, since today's readers often associate "rhetoric" with speech that gets its way dishonestly. That there is no easy response, or perhaps no response at all, to this modern doubt about Paul is indicated by the undeniable similarity between his self-revelations in 1:8 (and in 7:8–12) and the contemporary rhetoric of domestic violence: "I know I hurt you; it pains me that I hurt you; but I only wanted to show my love; I will harm myself if you do not forgive me." Rhetorical analysis cannot by itself determine whether Paul meant what he said, only how it *might* have been heard by a first-century audience.

2 Corinthians 1:15–2:4

If I Am a Flatterer, Then So Is God

The Text in Its Ancient Context

A pattern in Paul's argumentation is emerging. Paul's style of ministry mimics God's; his emotions are indistinguishable from Christ's. To fault him is to fault God. To oppose him is to oppose Christ. In this passage Paul deflects the super-apostles' charge of flattery by implicating God in the same yes-saying that he, Silvanus, and Timothy make the core of their preaching (for the "light touch" in 1:17 as a sign of flattery see Plutarch, *How to Tell a Flatterer from a Friend* 65B; 71F). The topic of flattery here is not in question, since from Cicero (*De amicitia* 93) we learn that the phrase "Yes, yes and No, no" had broad circulation as early as the first century BCE. It was a proverbial expression for the flatterer's malleability and desire to please and had been lifted from its original literary context of a play by Terence. The flatterer is devious; he wins victims over by posing as a friend and telling them what they want to hear. Flatterers transform themselves into the ones they seek to please, a behavior Paul's adaptability in 1 Cor. 9:19–23 dangerously approaches. Paul, however, argues that his change of travel plans (1:15–16) is not evidence of flattery but proof of his desire to spare the church further grief, a point he reiterates in 1:23–2:4.

In 1:18–22, Paul presents himself and God not as flatterers, though they do say only "yes," but as friends, as the term *pistos* ("faithful") in verse 18 and the verb *bebaioō* (lit., "I make firm or constant") in verse 21 indicate. These two terms were commonly associated with the motif of friendship (see Xenophon, *Memorabilia* 2.6.20; and Lucian, *Toxaris* 6–7, 9, 20, 35, 63) and now in Paul's use define the relationship of God with the community and the community with Paul.

The Text in the Interpretive Tradition

What did the early church make of Paul's letter of tears (2:4)? John Chrysostom made a proposal that persuaded many later commentators: the letter of tears is actually 1 Corinthians. Chrysostom thought the offender mentioned in 2 Cor. 2:5–11 was the same person singled out for discipline in 1 Cor. 5:1. While this solution has several obvious deficiencies, which modern commentaries do not fail to point out, one cannot keep from admiring its simplicity. But the chief problem with the proposal is this: in 1 Corinthians, Paul does not present himself as grieving. There is no reason to categorize it as a grieving letter (*epistolē lypētikē*).

The Text in Contemporary Discussion

Some scholars have suggested that we look no further than 2 Corinthians 10-13 to find Paul's "letter of tears" (see Watson). This would be a simple solution if it were not the case that in this portion of the letter Paul does not present himself as grieving, aside from the possibility of lament he mentions in 12:31. Furthermore, the "letter of tears" dealt with an individual's unjust act, but 2 Corinthians 10-13 concerns the super-apostles' rivalry with Paul. (For additional reasons to doubt identification of the "letter of tears" with chapters 10-13, see Amador.)

2 Corinthians 2:5–11

Shame and Satan

The Text in Its Ancient Context

This passage is the gateway to the rest of 2 Corinthians 1–7. Later arguments are anticipated as Paul seeks to persuade the community to forgive and accept the offender who had been disciplined and put to shame. Paul turns the injury from himself (2:5, 10) and stresses that now the community must forgive and confirm love. Here Paul is performing, and asking the church to enact, the inconsistency that the super-apostles perceive in Paul's ministry. A true apostle, they would assert, is severe (see 13:3), and the true church would enforce discipline without reprieve. But Paul detects the bullying and begrudging Satan (2:11) in such a one-sided approach to pastoral care. Paul sees the face of Christ, however, in the act of forgiveness (2:10). And then, in order to ground his ministry in Christ's lordship (which does not exclude weakness) and God's grace, Paul takes his readers on an extensive literary digression in 2:12–7:4, which echoes his painful procession to reunite with Titus in Macedonia.

The Text in the Interpretive Tradition

Paul's characterization of Satan as an envious bully (2 Cor. 2:11) would become a stock theme in early Christianity. Envy (!) entered the garden to corrupt Adam and Eve and their descendants (see Theophilus, *Ad Autolycum* 2.29; Epiphanius, *Panarion* 3.416.1; Antiochus Monachus, *Pandecta scripturae sacrae* 55). In this regard, there is an intriguing overlap in Christian and Hellenistic traditions as they grow and influence one another in late antiquity. Envy, understood as begrudging the happiness of another, was a prominent *theological* explanation among Greeks for human disappointment and loss (see Plutarch, *Consolatio ad Apollonium* 105B). In erotic relationships, personified Envy was blamed for separations (see Chariton, *Chareas and Callirhoe* 1.1.16; Nicetas Eugenianus, *Drosilla and Charicles* 1.52–53).

The Text in Contemporary Discussion

Readers interested in connecting Paul's concern about the shaming and isolating effects of punishment with current criticism of the American criminal justice system might consult the recently adopted social statement of the Evangelical Lutheran Church in America (see "The Church and Criminal Justice: Hearing the Cries," at http://www.elca.org/en/Faith/Faith-and-Society/Social-Statements/Criminal-Justice). The complicity of some Christian beliefs in the needless worsening of offenders' lives is slowly coming into general consciousness. For centuries, Christians have promoted biblical texts that view the purpose of punishment to be the isolation and destruction of offenders (see, e.g., 2 Peter). Christians elect state and federal legislators who pass laws requiring or enabling mass incarceration, mandatory sentencing, the location of prisons far removed from families and other systems of support, solitary confinement, and other collateral punishments that work through the harsh logic of isolation. It is sobering to think that Paul regards the self-destructive results of enforced isolation as the work of Satan.

2 Corinthians 2:12–3:3

Topography of an Apostle's Heart

The Text in Its Ancient Context

This is a provocative definition of the rhetorical unit since, as I noted above, many scholars detect a seam between verses 13 and 14. They suggest that 2:14–7:5 (with the possible exception of 6:14–7:1) was taken from another Pauline epistle and inserted into an opening created by cutting between 2:13 and what is now 7:5. Attractive as this theory might be (it accounts for what would otherwise be a delayed thanksgiving period in 2:14), there are thematic continuities that make the proposal of interpolation unnecessary. Note the place names in verses 12–13 (Troas and Macedonia) and Paul's reference to "every place" in verse 14. Along these lines, the term *thriambeuein* ("to lead in triumphal procession") suggests movement, while in verses 12–13 Paul discuss his travel in some detail. But the most striking connection between the writing before and after the conjectured seam is the resonance between Paul's having "no relief" at not finding Titus and the apostle's being led in a triumphal procession. A brief explanation of the Roman triumph, and of its adaptation by ancient erotic writers (primarily in poetry and ancient romance), is in order.

Roman generals had the practice of degrading foreign nobility captured in military campaigns by parading them as slaves through the streets of Rome. For poets and novelists, Eros conquered, enslaved, and forced the rejected lover, or the one uncertain of the beloved's response, to march in an equally humiliating procession (see Ovid, *Amores* 1.2.19–52; and Miller). Two other motifs, both of which figure prominently in 2 Corinthians, were often allied with the lover led in triumph. *Servitium amoris* (the slavery of love; see Murgatroyd) depicted the lover's paradoxical "voluntary slavery" (e.g., Plato, *Symposium* 184C), degrading loss of self-control (Zagagi), and lovesickness even to the point of death (Xenophon, *Symposium* 4.14; Achilles Tatius, *Leucippe and Clitophon* 1.7.2–3). Paul deploys the other popular motif,

Amor vincit omnia ("Love conquers all"), in 2:14 and extensively in 2 Corinthians 10-13.

So, how does Paul turn the erotic connotations of the triumph motif to his rhetorical aim of conciliating the Corinthians to himself? The metaphor presents Paul suffering a lover's pain, the grief of separation from his beloved community, and, more significantly, apprehension over its response to his stinging reproof in the letter of tears. He presents himself suffering with self-accusation and worry, not unlike the unrequited lover of Latin elegy, whose every thought is about the beloved's rejection. Moreover, note that *God* leads Paul in this triumphal procession. This is striking not only because readers knew that Eros plays the part of conquering general in love poetry but even more because knowledge of God is apparent for all who see into Paul's experience, which he has been narrating since "our affliction" in 1:4. Some, of course, will smell nothing but the odor of death; presumably Paul wants readers to think of the super-apostles here. Paul's readers, however, *if and as they remain true to him*, will perceive the fragrance of life in his socially demeaning and soul-draining love for them.

The Text in the Interpretive Tradition

For over a thousand years, "Love conquers all" lay dormant, but when it awoke in the Middle Ages it was applied to Pauline texts with vigor. Even God is vanquished by love for humanity, according to Bernard of Clairvaux (*Sermon* 64.10 [PL 183:1088]). Hadewijch of Antwerp thought so too.

> *What seems to the loved soul the most beautiful encounter*
> *Is that it should love the Beloved so fully*
> *And so gain knowledge of the Beloved with love*
> *That nothing else is known by it*
> *Except: "I am conquered by Love"*
> *But he who overcame Love was rather conquered*

So that he might in love be brought to naught
God the lover is victim of love. (Poems in Stanzas *8.71–77)*

In the fourteenth century, the Byzantine theologian Nicholas Cabasilas, writing about the christological topic of *kenosis* ("emptying"), likens the God emptied by *erōs* first to the "locked out lover," perhaps the most popular ancient cliché depicting the slave of love, and then to the "lover led in a triumphal procession" (*thriambeuein erastēn*: *The Life in Christ* 6.3). Even though it took over a thousand years, the erotic motif of triumph in 2 Cor. 2:14 opened a way into the passion of God that had been foreclosed by the philosophically inspired doctrine of divine impassibility.

2 Corinthians 3:1–18

Frank Speech and Moses' Face

The Text in Its Ancient Context

This section is a carefully crafted argument resting to a great degree on Paul's playfulness with the Greek language, and therefore difficult to appreciate in English translation. Nevertheless, some points can be made. In 3:12, Paul claims to use the very *parrēsia* ("frank" or "free speech," not "boldness" as the NRSV translates; see Fredrickson 1996) that his opponents charge that he lacks. Paul's rhetorical predicament lies in the fact that he makes this claim at a distance, through a letter; for Paul simply to assert his free speech would be to confirm the criticism directed against him. His solution is this: rather than giving proof of his confidence based on his own power (3:5), Paul appeals to the Spirit, whose work was to inscribe the Corinthians in his heart (3:2–3; for the eroticism of such writing, see *Greek Anthology* 12.57).

The Spirit is life-making precisely in this way, by its deepening of *philia* ("friendship") to the point of love (*erōs* or *agapē*). *Parrēsia* of this kind is the language of friendship, as Plutarch once remarked (*How to Tell a Flatterer from a Friend* 51C), not the verbal expression of an individual's freedom attained through self-control and moral accomplishment, as many philosophers (and most likely the super-apostles) taught. If *parrēsia* is a function of friendship, Paul argues, then the new covenant (literally "new arrangement"), which is love and longing for communion kindled by gazing at another's face and being looked upon (cf. 1 Cor. 13:12), guarantees free speech to all, wherever the Spirit is. The covenant of death, though having a glory of its own, is the application of written laws and commands; it does not create friendship and is unable to kindle the gaze upon the face of another and experience the other in his or her singularity, as the sons of Israel discover (3:7).

Moses' face plays an equally important role in the second of the proofs of Paul's *parrēsia* (3:12–18). The argument here is structured according to the rhetorical technique of comparison (*synkrisis*), using negative and positive examples. Paul is not like Moses, who covered his face, a movement in Greek culture associated with shame. Moses veiled his face so that the "sons of Israel" might not gaze upon the *telos* ("end," in the sense of intended result) of "that which is being nullified," presumably the old covenant. The shaming effect of that which is written on stone was alluded to in 3:9 in two ways. First, the word Paul uses to describe the end result of the new covenant, *glory*, was generally understood as the opposite of shame. Second, the old covenant is described as a ministry of condemnation. It is tempting to think that Paul is describing the situation of the disciplined offender in 2:5–11. He, Moses, the "sons of Israel" (3:14–15), and perhaps Paul himself—as he made his way through Asia to Macedonia, despairing of life over the alienation he feared his *grammata* ("letters") had worked on the Corinthian church—they are all caught up in the ministry of death.

But Moses' face does not remain veiled. Verse 16 should be translated, "whenever he [not "one"] turned to the Lord, the veil was taken away." The "he" is Moses in his role as positive example. Paul, indeed the whole church, is *just like* Moses, who in that moment of face-to-face intimacy with the Lord, an intimacy created by the Spirit, is free, and if free, then bold of speech, since the two words *eleutheria* and *parrēsia* were nearly synonymous. So once again Paul bases his free speech not on individual power or accomplishment but on a Spirit-made intimacy in which "we all" (3:18) are free in the moment of an uncovered face, as in the climactic instant of the ancient Greek wedding when the bride—her veil swept aside in the moment of *apokalypsis*—and groom gazed without shame on each other's face. The political consequences of 3:18 are staggering when contrasted with the ancient world's limitation of freedom and frank speech to elite male citizens. In the phrase "we all," Paul envisions a community of any and all persons, all equally free to speak their minds, as they simultaneously gaze upon one another as if in a mirror and in this way are transformed into what they see, Christ the image of God (cf. 4:4).

The Text in the Interpretive Tradition

"For the letter kills, but the Spirit gives life" (3:6). No other Pauline phrase so profoundly set the course of Christian biblical interpretation and theology. Early on, Paul's distinction between letter and Spirit, in which he clearly prefers Spirit over letter, was interpreted as the difference between text and the author's intention (see Grant). At least three consequences flowed from this reading: first, it paved the way for the phonocentrism of Greek philosophy to overtake Christian theology. What is phonocentrism? Jacques Derrida has analyzed texts in the Western intellectual tradition, from Plato (see especially *Phaedrus* 275C–276E) to the twentieth century, and has pointed out the tradition's unjustified preference for voice over writing. Yet it is not Derrida's point simply to reverse the two by awarding to writing a privileged status over voice. Rather, he shows that what philosophers understand as the deficiencies (Derrida would not use this term) of writing affect the voice as well, but very few thinkers ever admit this. For example, it is generally agreed that writing inevitably destabilizes meaning, since the mortality of the author and that of the reader leave no enduring witness to what was meant when the text was composed. The move that characterizes phonocentrism is to claim that the everyday experience of hearing oneself think or the perceived immediacy of speaking one's thoughts proves that voice mitigates the danger of contaminating one's thoughts. The voice holds and protects the idea from contamination, so it is claimed in phonocentrism, as it travels from one's mind through the external world through another's ear and ultimately to his or her own interiority. In short, phonocentrism thinks of voice as a somewhat successful substitute for the thinking one does silently in one's head; but writing, in this view, as a phonetic system representing voice in the speaker's absence, is merely a substitute for a substitute and thus two steps removed from self-present thought (see Culler, 89–110). From the phonocentric perspective, then, the letter kills in the sense that it fails to live up to the voice's power to deliver the speaker's thoughts. Second, the misconstrued distinction between letter and Spirit enabled Christians to appropriate the allegorical method employed by Stoics (and others) in the interpretation of Homer and thus created a special class of spiritual persons who presumed they could read past the literal meaning of texts into God's mind. Third, the distinction between letter and Spirit contributes to animosity against Jews, who, according to the Christian interpretation of Paul's distinction, are incapable of knowing the meaning of their own Scriptures.

The Text in Contemporary Discussion

Paul's reasoning from friendship and the face here bears an intriguing resemblance to recent approaches to ethics by writers influenced by Jacques Derrida and Emmanuel Levinas (see, e.g., Caputo 1993; for the related idea of *perichōrēsis* in recent trinitarian theology and ecclesiology, see Moltmann 2000). Nevertheless, Derrida's wariness of the reduction of friendship to brotherhood in Western political philosophy, which buys the communion of some at the price of excluding others, must be kept in mind (Derrida). Does Paul himself fall into the trap of building a community on the backs of others, that is, on the exclusion of "the sons of Israel" (3:7)? This question, which can only be raised here and not answered, is crucial in light of the comparison Paul makes between the two covenants in 3:4–18. It is not possible to rescue Paul from the charge of anti-Judaism simply by pointing out that it is the old covenant that is nullified (3:14) and not Judaism itself. Is there a difference between covenant and Judaism, or enough of a difference between the two so that Christ's nullification of the former does not mean the destruction of the latter?

2 Corinthians 4:1–6

Your Slaves

The Text in Its Ancient Context

In 4:1–3, Paul reiterates his claim that he possesses all the boldness and openness necessary for an apostle of Christ, and if anyone (think super-apostles here) thinks his gospel is hidden or that he is playing tricks on the Corinthians with his talk of grace and forgiveness, then it must be that the god of this age (think Satan here) has blinded their minds. A word about the two major ancient theories of vision might be helpful at this point. One theory, which posits that very small bits of objects break off and pass through the air into the soul via the eyes, plays no role here. The other imagines a light in the soul or mind, burning like a lamp and sending out its rays through the eyes to illumine external objects. From this latter perspective, to be blinded is to have one's internal fire extinguished. That is what Paul says the god of this age has done to his opponents. They have no fire. In them, no beams of light proceed from an internal fire, and this suggests that they lack love or desire, which was also conceptualized as burning within the innards (cf. 1 Cor. 7:9; 2 Cor. 11:29). They do not love the Corinthians as Paul does; rather, Paul implies, they preach themselves as lords over the community (cf. 2 Cor. 1:24; 11:20).

In contrast, Paul preaches himself as the community's slave (4:5). Paul once more alludes to the *servitium amoris* motif so popular in the erotic literature of the ancient world (see comments on 2:14 above). He loves the Corinthians madly and without regard for his own dignity, and he does so in imitation of Jesus ("on account of Jesus"), who took the form of a slave (see Phil. 2:7).

The Text in the Interpretive Tradition

The Christian tradition by and large has suppressed Paul's vision of a lovesick, servile Christ who is here Paul's model for imitation. The authors of Colossians and Ephesians, for example, eliminated the motif of Christ as slave as they revised Paul's theology and substituted their philosophically influenced gospel of self-control. But there are moments in the tradition when poetry returns Christology to Paul's daring appropriation of the slavery motif, which we find in Phil. 2:7 as well. Guerric of Igny (1080-1157) is a good example of a writer turning Christ's slavery away from obedience to God the Father and toward humanity.

> "I will not serve," man says to his Creator. "Then I will serve you," his Creator says to man. "You sit down. I will minister, I will wash your feet. You rest; I will bear your weariness, your infirmities. Use me as you like in all your needs, not only as your slave but also as your beast of burden and as your property." (*Sermon* 29.1; Monks of Mount Saint Bernard Abbey, 2:55–56)

At the end of the thirteenth century or the beginning of the fourteenth, the Italian mystic Jacopone da Todi spoke to Jesus in a way that likely would not have displeased Paul.

> *You went about the world as if you were drunk,*
> *Led by Love as if you were a slave . . .*

The Text in Contemporary Discussion

Paul's introduction of slavery into his discourse about Christ and about his own ministry have not gone unnoticed by contemporary scholars.

Some quite correctly criticize the way the idea of Jesus as a slave (to God, as it is almost always assumed) has legitimated various forms of domination within the church and in secular social institutions influenced by Christianity (Briggs). Recognition that the figure of the popular leader (demagogue) in ancient democracies was frequently described in servile terms (Martin 1990) goes some distance in undermining the oppressive potential of this motif. For many other scholars, however, Jesus' slavery to God is not at all problematic—quite the opposite, since they think his obedience as the "new Adam" reverses the disobedience of the first Adam, thereby offering salvation and a model of Christian behavior to the church (see Barth, 63–64).

The erotic motif of *servitium amoris* in 2 Cor. 4:5 and throughout the epistle has important consequences for the interpretation of Paul's Christology, understanding his hopes for the political culture of the churches he established and, ultimately, the contemporary appropriation of Pauline thought for contemporary Christianity. First, the "work of Christ" (a standard phrase used by theologians to speak of the role of Jesus in their theological systems) will have to include his passionate longing for communion, his slave-like devotion to humanity. Second, church leaders, who often claim to pattern themselves after Paul, would have to question the prevalent view of Paul as an authoritarian leader and imitate instead his imitation of Christ as a slave of love. Finally, ecclesiastical regimes of oppression that legitimate themselves by an appeal to Jesus' obedience to the Father, or in the case of secular institutions by obedience to higher authority, would have to be challenged (see Fredrickson 2013).

2 Corinthians 4:7–5:10

More Body

The Text in Its Ancient Context

To review: in the face of charges that he is a deceptive flatterer lacking courage to speak his mind, Paul asserts his *parrēsia* (3:12, 4:1), placing it in the context of friendship and love but also contrasting it with the speech of the super-apostles who, like the Cynics, are harsh moral critics. In 4:7–5:10, he further develops the idea of frank speaking based on friendship. In language that anticipates the weakness he will describe as his experience in the aftermath of his abduction into paradise in 12:1–10, Paul's hardships in 4:8–12 remind him that the power he possesses in excess is not the force of command but the enslaving power of love, which God has enkindled in his heart to illumine the glory of God that Paul sees on the face of Christ (4:6). The slavery motif is developed in 4:10–12, where the bearing of the master's death in one's own body goes to the heart of servitude, as verse 12 powerfully states. Paul's *servitium amoris* to Christ is inseparable from his slavery to the church in Corinth. It is out of this relationship with the church, not his own moral virtue, that his speech flows freely (4:13).

The topic of 4:14–5:10 is increased intimacy in the *parrēsia*-generating relationship Paul has with the Corinthians. He begins in 4:14–15 by repeating the topics of resurrection and transformation (see 1:10–11, 14, 21; 3:18). Abruptly, however, as if Paul had a conversion to the philosophic doctrine of the immortality of the soul, 4:16–5:1 introduces stock themes about the afterlife as it was described in Platonism and accepted by a few of the later Stoics. These themes include the inner and outer human being; the insignificance of present suffering in comparison with the soul's perfection; the eternality of things unseen; and, most significantly, the body as prison or temporary dwelling place of the soul (See Seneca, *Ep*. 102.23; 120.14). New Testament scholars have for decades pointed out the profound difference between immortality of the soul and resurrection of the body. So why has Paul conflated the two notions here? Quite possibly Paul speaks like a philosopher in 4:16–5:1 in order to undermine philosophy's commitment to the survival of the separated self that lives in unchanging and serene contemplation of the universe when the external influence of its body has been removed. By temporarily passing as a philosopher in 4:16–5:1, he gives his attack on philosophical reason all the advantages of stealth.

Having drawn his readers' attention to the isolated self-sufficiency of the wise man's soul (see 3:5), note in 5:2–5 how powerfully Paul rejects the philosophical idea of death as the soul stripped of flesh (see Seneca, *Ep.*102.24–25). He groans and longs for more clothing, for more body, not less. Life after death for Paul is not the eradication of death (that is philosophy's delusion in the teaching of the immortal, bodiless soul), but the drinking down of death by life (NRSV "swallowing up," cf. 1 Cor. 15:53–57), an unimaginable event and an impossible possibility (5:4) rightly given over by Paul to the name of God, who gives the Spirit (cf. 1:20–22).

The Text in the Interpretive Tradition

Interpreters up to the tenth century understood the "inner person" (4:16) as Paul's reference to the soul just as the "outer person" designated the body (Suda, *Lexicon* Epsilon 3170). Yet if it is the case, as discussed above, that Paul *plays* with the philosophical commonplace of body as the house (or prison, or crypt) of the soul in order to challenge the very notion of a bodiless soul, the interpreters of the early church and the Byzantine period mistook his rhetorical strategy in 4:16–5:1. They thought he was advocating asceticism as the path to spiritual perfection. In fact, with great regularity, they slightly misquoted the Pauline text as follows: "*as much as* the outer person is destroyed, *to this extent* the inner person is renewed" (emphasis mine: see Basil, *Quod deus non est auctor malorum* [PG 31:337]; Ephraem Syrus, *In sermonem, quem dixit dominus, quod: In hoc mundo pressuram habebitis, et de perfectione hominis* 335; Michael Choniates, *Epistulae* 2.132.269).

The Text in Contemporary Discussion

In recent years there has been a growing interest in possible intersections of Pauline thought and contemporary philosophy (see Caputo and Alcoff; Frick). Second Corinthians 4:16–5:10, in its complex engagement with Platonic themes, is a natural site for these modern conversations to take place. Three Pauline themes (there are certainly others) in this passage invite comparison with postmodern philosophy, which has its own complex engagement with Platonism that at least on some points runs parallel to Paul's. First, the thought of death swallowed down by life, discussed above, and the accompanying thought of resurrection did not fall on an unsympathetic ear in the case of Jacques Derrida (Kearney); indeed, for Derrida, dreaming the impossible is always the way to start any undertaking whatsoever, but especially in the case of philosophy, theology, and justice (see Caputo 1997, 20–26). Second, the famous Pauline phrase "for we walk by faith not by sight" (5:7) reads almost as a motto for some postmodern critiques of foundationalism (Caputo 1997, 41–48). Third, the eschatological desire for a future that cannot be known or described is indicated by the groaning, longing, and wishing of 5:2, and this passion correlates with the aim of deconstruction: to impassion a wish for something totally other in those of us whom tradition, theology, and social systems have trained not to expect the unexpected and not to welcome surprises (Caputo 1997, 134–49).

2 Corinthians 5:11–19

The Madness of Saint Paul

The Text in Its Ancient Context

In 5:13, Paul admits that he went insane (*exestēmen*), a moment of candor whose significance is not apparent. The present essay has stressed Paul's consistent description of the opponents' Cynic-like moral severity and their complaint against him that he is bold in letters but deceptively weak in the church's presence. If this is the situation, then 5:13 might be read as Paul's admission of inconsistency and his explanation of it. Going mad with violent emotion in rhetorical performance was, in fact, an important element in the style of speech called *deinotēs* (see the comments above on 2 Cor. 10:9–10; and Voit), and presumably the opponents would have approved of Paul's blast of anger in the letter of tears. The style of speech contrasting with *deinotēs* was known as "grace" (*charis*). To achieve this style, the speaker must do precisely what Paul says he did when he returned from his madness and is still doing as he writes: "we are temperate" (*sōphronoumen*: see Van Hook, 32). The purpose of this calm self-presentation was to persuade and win over (as Paul says he aims to do in 5:11) rather than to overwhelm hearers as in the case of *deinotēs*.

Following on Paul's confession of madness are two applications of the motif of friendship, one to Christ (5:14–17) and the other to God (5:18–19). In each instance, the point is to distance Paul's ministry from flattery and associate it as closely as possible with divine grace (cf. 1:12). The "love [*agapē*] of Christ" in 5:14 will be misunderstood if readers interpret it through the influential but problematic work of Anders Nygren's *Agape and Eros*, which rules out of order the porous border between *agapē* and *philia* running throughout the present commentary (for a trenchant critique of Nygren, see McGinn). There is one point about friendship in antiquity, however, that Nygren properly underlines: its exclusivity. There was in Paul's day the widespread opinion that friendship was dyadic; if anyone had more than one, or possibly two friends, that person might well be thought of as a flatterer and guilty of *polyphilia*, the vice of having many friends (see Plutarch, *On Having Many Friends* 93B–97B). Read against this aversion to *polyphilia*, the quasi-hymnic writing in 5:14–15 trades on the commonplace that "friends have all things in common" (how else would all die or all live unless all share all things with Christ?). There is a "new creation" (5:17) in which having many friends is the very nature of things, not a symptom of flattery and deception.

Paul shifts in 5:18–19 from a christo-logic to a theo-logic, but the point remains the same. The new, many-friended creature that Paul is legitimates his manner of ministry in which reconciliation (in the sense defined below) and forgiveness take center stage. This new creation applies to God also, although interpreters rarely notice this. The Greek word translated "reconcile" does not refer to a restoration of a previous relationship so much as the initiation of new friendship (see Fredrickson

1997, 171–74) in which all things are shared. God's yes-saying in Christ (1:18–20) is matched by God's having all things in common with the *kosmos* and placing in "us" (Paul? Paul and his cowriters? the readers, too? the world?) the *logos* (word? logic?) of reconciliation.

The Text in the Interpretive Tradition

Various commentators have wanted to protect Paul from the meaning of his own words. Typical is John Chrysostom, who rendered the sense of Paul's statement hypothetical: "What Paul means is that *even if* people think he is mad, everything he does is for the glory of God" (*Homilies on the Epistles of Paul to the Corinthians* 11.2, emphasis added). Other interpreters have construed Paul's madness as prophetic truth-telling, since they read *exestēmen* in 5:13 in light of Ps. 116:11: "I said in my consternation [*en tē ekstasei mou*] 'Everyone is a liar'" (see Eusebius, *Commentaria in Psalmos* [PG 23:353]). The latter reading supports the explanation given above. Finally, in the early church there was another interpretation of Paul's madness, and this one plays an important role in present-day discussions. It is that 2 Cor. 5:13 refers to Paul's vision of the Lord recounted in 12:1–10 (see Athanasius, *Expositiones in Psalmos* [PG 27:301]; and Cyril of Alexandria, *Expositio in Psalmos* [PG 69:1156]).

The Text in Contemporary Discussion

Paul's madness (5:13) is difficult to understand. An influential explanation among today's scholarly readers is that Paul's opponents, influenced by Gnosticism or by the ideal of the "divine man," had accused him of *not* having ecstatic experiences, validations in their view of an apostle of Christ (Schmithals, 187–89; Georgi, 252, 280–83). This verse would thus be Paul's rebuttal. As we have seen, there is indeed support in the early church for one portion of this claim, Paul's possible allusion to visionary experience. Yet the larger assertion, that a demand had been placed on Paul, depends on our viewing the opponents as seekers of ecstatic visions or speaking in tongues, for which there is scant evidence in 2 Corinthians and silence in the interpretive tradition (see Barrett 1973, 166–67; Furnish, 324–25).

2 Corinthians 5:20–7:4

God Entreating through Us, Not Them

The Text in Its Ancient Context

In a tender and urgent reminiscence of 1:3–7, where it was likewise not possible to distinguish between God's entreaty or exhortation and Paul's, so also in 5:20–6:2 Paul pleads for the community to be reconciled (in the full sense of the term) to him. If the Corinthians withhold forgiveness, then Paul's ministry itself becomes the cause of offense (6:2) in spite of the proof of its validity provided by the hardships he suffers (6:4–10). With an open mouth (6:11), an allusion to *parrēsia* (see Isocrates, *Oration* 12.96), he entreats the church, calling them by name ("Corinthians"). His heart is wide, a sign of joy and the holding of another in one's heart as in 3:2–3. Holding another in one's heart is a sign of friendship, according to John Chrysostom (PG 61:491), but the community's grief has narrowed (6:12) their souls (see Diogenes Laertius, *Lives of Illustrious Philosophers* 7.118) and forced Paul out of their "innards" (*tois splanchnois*). He pleads with them (6:13) to make room for him.

Paul then pleads with the church in Corinth not to align itself with the super-apostles. Scholars have correctly identified "mismatched" (*heterozygountes*) as nuptial imagery. Their assessment is confirmed by the terms denoting union, which follow in verses 15–16, especially *koinōnia*, which was widely employed; marriage was defined, in fact, as a *koinōnia* of bodies, wealth, and children. And yet the way the same scholars deal with *apistois* (translated by the NRSV as "with unbelievers") leads them to conclude that Paul here warns church members not to marry outside the community (cf. 1 Cor. 7:12–16 for a more complex view on the matter held by Paul himself). There is another way to read this text. The term *apistos* in 4:4 likely refers to the *disloyal* super-apostles. Moreover, not only did the yoke (*zygos*) function in marital contexts, but it was also a metaphor for the pulling together of friends. Paul uses it in Phil. 4:3 to persuade the readers of that letter to financially support the missionary work of Euodia and Syntyche as the church had supported him. Paul's plea, then, not to be "otherwise-yoked" with the unfaithful ones might be interpreted as his warning not to support the super-apostles.

The Text in the Interpretive Tradition

Interpreters in the early church sometimes found themselves in the uncomfortable position of making sense of texts that, from the perspective of the tradition's adherence to the *apatheia* (impassibility) of God, could not mean what they say. "The word *became* flesh" (emphasis added) in John 1:14 is a good example. Here the threat to the unchangeable, eternal Word comes not from heretical teaching but from the biblical text itself. The recourse of substituting "take on flesh" for "become flesh" was the preferred solution to this problem (see Theodoret of Cyrus, *Eranistes*, passim). Another famous example is Gal. 3:13, where we read that Christ "became a curse for us"; Jerome explained (*Commentarius in Epistolam S. Pauli ad Galatas* 2 [PL26:387–88]) that this should not be taken literally—to Luther's irritation (*Lectures on Galatians* [*LW* 26:276]).This brings us to 2 Cor. 5:21, which Athanasius (*Oratio II contraArianos* 47.2) recognized was as problematic as John 1:14 and Gal. 3:13. The stakes are high, however, since this verse undergirds Paul's plea for reconciliation in 5:20 and presents readers with a shocking idea: God made Christ "to be sin." Gregory of Nyssa (*Contra Celsum* 1.69) softened the offense by claiming that Paul wrote *sin* but meant *flesh*. Eutherius (*Confutationes quarundam propositionum* 4) took a different approach and applied what interpreters in the tradition had learned in dealing with John 1:14: Christ was not altered to be sin but "took our sin and caused it to disappear" (*aphanisai*). Theodorus Studites (*Parva Catechesis* 30) similarly emphasized that Christ "put on" human nature corrupted by sin.

The Text in Contemporary Discussion

What do love (*agapē*, 5:14) and justice (*dikaiosynē*, 5:21) have to do with one another? This important question, especially in the context of Christian responses to the criminal justice system in the United States, has been sidelined by Nygren's approach to love and by translators insisting on using "righteousness" to represent *dikaiosynē*. Even when the question is asked, however, justice is often reduced to calculation or the equitable enforcement of rules, and love is reduced to mercy's smoothing the rough edges of justice. But Paul holds the two tightly together, each indeed as an example of the other, not only in 2 Corinthians 5 but also in Gal. 5:5–6 and, by extension through nuptial imagery, in Phil. 3:7–11. Justice and love share at least two things in Paul. First, each is constituted by openness to the future (see especially Gal. 5:5–6). Just as one would never say of a beloved, "I have loved enough," so justice forbids saying, "justice has been done." The second thing love and justice share is that they spring from the singularity of the other; it is always the face of *this one* that calls forth my love just as it is the call of *this one* that moves me to response. For these reasons, both love and justice are pure gifts.

2 Corinthians 8:1–9:15

By Poverty Enriched

The Text in Its Ancient Context

In the ancient world, gift-giving displayed social status and obligated recipients to repay benefactors with gratitude and honor (see Danker). While Paul challenges the elite of the Corinthian church in these two chapters to contribute to the fund for the saints in Jerusalem, he nevertheless seeks to persuade them not to participate in a system of benefaction that would shame the poor in the Corinthian church (since they had nothing to give) and would establish the churches of Greece and Asia as patrons of the struggling client church in Jerusalem. Paul has a difficult task in front of him: to disrupt the circle of gift and gratitude without ruining the collection itself.

Paul shames the Corinthians by praising the generosity of the impoverished Macedonians (8:1–6). Yet there is more to it than this. First, an impossible logic about the Macedonian gift loosens, if not dissolves, the connection between giving and the display of social status. How so? In verse 2, the strange condition that makes gift-giving possible is "profound poverty." It is not the case, then, as it is with Corinth's wealthy elite, that the Macedonians give out of their fullness, as if their gift testified to their invulnerability. Like the widow in Mark 12:41–44, the Macedonians give out of their emptiness.

In 8:9, the "gift [*charis*] of our Lord Jesus Christ" follows the same unexpected pattern of giving out of poverty, in language that echoes the Christ hymn in Phil. 2:5–11. Paul writes, "by the poverty of that one you got rich." Next, in 8:13–15, Paul tries a second strategy, manipulating the well-known philosophical topic of proportional equality (Aristotle, *Nicomachean Ethics* 1130b–1132b). Instead of the expected notion of equality as distribution according to status (that is, equality is achieved when superior persons receive more), however, Paul implies that the very act of giving is the admission that one might one day be in need. Equality understood in this way exposes human frailty, even that of the elite, within any system of economic exchange.

To the ears of modern readers, chapter 9 simply repeats chapter 8. One prominent scholar has argued that the two chapters circulated independently before the final compilation of 2 Corinthians (see Betz). But to repeat oneself was not necessarily a fault in ancient letters (see Phil. 3:1). And although it is the case in chapter 9 that Paul again undermines the patron-client structure that had monopolized the act of giving in the ancient world, he does so in a different way, using a theological argument: God's justice *is* God's scattering, and this is good news for the poor, as the quotation of the Psalm in 9:9 suggests. Such a definition of justice (NRSV translates "righteousness") must have been shocking, since in the wake of Plato (*Republic* 433B–435B), justice was understood as a harmony of interests or a strict limitation on individuals to perform assigned roles within an unchallenged gradation of social power. In short, 2 Corinthians 8 and 9 does not credit God with preserving the patron-client relationship, but with deconstructing it. The wildly unaccountable dissemination in verses 10–11, just another instance of scattering, does indeed produce gratitude to God, but what is one to be grateful for (note the "indescribable gift" in 9:15) at the scene of such dispersion accomplished by God's giving? Might it be the generosity (*haplotēs*), made possible by God's grace, of shaking things loose? Thus, in the end, it is not gratitude that Paul imagines the poor in Jerusalem will feel toward the church in Corinth: it is longing for communion (vv. 13–14).

The Text in Contemporary Discussion

Paul's probing of the ideology of the gift (*charis*), which might also be translated as "grace," bears a remarkable resemblance to recent philosophical and theological discussions of gift-giving (see Horner; Walters) that have been inspired, at least in part, by Derrida's critical analysis of Marcel Mauss's 1925 anthropological study *The Gift: The Form and Reason for Exchange in Archaic Societies*. What is the connection between the first-century apostle and recent philosophers, at least the ones for whom the language of religion has proven indispensable? Very briefly stated, for Derrida, the gift in a pure sense is impossible: it refuses to let itself be intended by the giver or perceived by the recipient. In the moment that a gift either generates the expectation of repayment or a feeling of obligation, it ceases to be a gift. Thus the very possibility of a gift (for which there needs to exist a giver, a gift, and a recipient) also makes gift-giving impossible (see Caputo 1997, 160–64). This is not a mere word game, as Paul's ingenious and impassioned attempt to free the collection from the ancient system of benefaction shows. Christ's poverty, God's disseminative justice, and the gift's indescribability all reflect Paul's efforts to keep the elite from capitalizing on the collection and dominating the Corinthian church.

2 Corinthians 10:1–18

Miles Gloriosus: Militia Amoris

The Text in Its Ancient Context

In the first five words of 10:1, Paul manages to say "I" three times and to write "Paul" once for good measure. His audacity, mentioned in 7:16 but kept under wraps in chapters 8 and 9, now bursts forth: Paul is a warrior! But unlike the stock figure of the *milesgloriosus* of Roman comedy (see Plautus, *The Swaggering Soldier*), whose penchant for comparing himself to others and commending himself (see 10:12–18) sets the stage for Paul's appearance in chapters 10-12, and in whose image Paul creates the super-apostles, Paul is a soldier in Love's campaign. Rather than boasting in personal power, he swaggers in his weakness (10:10; 11; 21, 29, 12:9–10; 13:3–4, 9). This is not, however, weakness in a general sense, that is, an incapacity that could be remedied with extra effort or training. Rather, the erotic motifs woven into the discourse of these chapters suggest that Paul's weakness is the kind ancient love poets wrote about: desire for a communion that appears impossible. Second Corinthians 10-13 is a complex argument, ironies captured within ironies, a pretended and demented bragging about those desperate emotions about which no one but a crazed lover would ever boast. Paul's boasting in his weakness was intended to expose his opponents' severity and to commend Christ's gentleness and reasonableness that the apostle seeks to emulate.

Once again, the charge of duplicity rears its head: 10:1 incorporates into its own discourse the opponents' complaint that Paul is bold at a distance but *tapeinos* ("lowly," connoting, from the perspective of elites, marginalized persons of low social class) when present. Fighting words! Note the military terms marching forward: "I am bold" (10:2), "daring" (10:2), "wage war" (10:3), "weapons of our warfare" (10:4), "take down strongholds" (10:4) and "elevated heights" (10:5), "taking captive" (10:5), "obedience" (10:5,6), and "avenge disobedience" (10:6). Paul is conducting a campaign, to be sure, but first-century readers, especially those who remembered the motif of the triumphal procession in 2:14 and its association with the motif *servitium amoris*, would see the amatory point: Paul portrays himself as Eros taking captive and subjecting to servitude the high-minded, philosophical despisers of love, who in ancient amatory literature often reversed course and fell especially hard in love through Eros's avenging intervention (see the opening chapter of Xenophon of Ephesus, *An Ephesian Tale*; Philostratus, *Ep.* 12; *Greek Anthology* 5.294). Verse 6 marks a pause in the general campaign; only when the Corinthians' obedience to Christ (obedience of love, that is, another instance of *servitium amoris*) is complete will Paul turn to the others. Yet, lest anyone take his feigned belligerence in 10:1–6 seriously, in 10:8 he denies intent to pull anything or anyone down. He wouldn't want to frighten anyone (10:9)!

The Text in the Interpretive Tradition

According to 10:9–10, Paul's letters written before 2 Corinthians had already entered an interpretive tradition of considerable sophistication. As I noted in the introduction, the super-apostles evaluated Paul's letters and speech according to the literary and rhetorical standards of the time; his speech in the presence of the community, they said (10:10), was "attenuated" (*exouthenēmenos*). The *Rhetorica ad Herennium* (4.11.16) equated attenuated speech with the simple style that employed everyday language and could, if handled skillfully, achieve elegance. If mishandled, however, it was debased and merely ordinary, and as Cicero noted (*Deoratore* 20; see also Quintilian, *Institutio oratoria* 9.2.3), it was furthest from the forceful style (*deinotēs*). In short, we might infer the opponents charged that Paul in the presence of the church used irony (*eirōneia*), not in the modern sense of saying the opposite of what one means but in the ancient sense. That is, he talked the way poor people and slaves talked (cf. 1 Cor. 1:28), although he was capable of much more, and did so in order to ridicule others (see Dio Chrysostom, *Oration* 42.1–3). John Chrysostom (*In illud: Utinam sustineretis modicum* [PG 51:304]) had no doubt that Paul's opponents accused him of irony. In fact, Chrysostom's reading of 2 Cor. 10:9–10, and particularly his detailed explanation of Paul's "attenuated speech," lines up with the discussion of this topic in rhetorical handbooks and literary treatises (for a deep appreciation of Chrysostom as a Pauline interpreter, see Mitchell).

The Text in Contemporary Discussion

Such talk about lowliness, weakness, love, and slavery in Christian discourse forced Friedrich Nietzsche to cry out, "Bad air! Bad air!" (Nietzsche, 24). Hatred, revenge, envy—these terms taken together translate *ressentiment*, the word Nietzsche deployed against what he perceived to be the stench of Jewish and Christian souls deformed by the "revaluation of values." In a "slave revolt," he complained, the weak of the world seek "spiritual revenge" against the strong and their spontaneous affirmation of life; by promoting guilt, pettiness, and duties, the priestly class prevails by sullying the heroic embrace of life (Nietzsche, 19–33). This is not the place to assert or deny that Paul's weakness or the *servitium amoris* motif were examples of *ressentiment*, but the question might at least be raised whether the eroticism Paul weaves into his self-presentation and into his Christology entails a spontaneous and infinite affirmation of the other and thus even a slight chance for a rapprochement with Nietzsche's "yes-saying." (For a reading of the philosopher that might facilitate such an unexpected meeting of minds, see Caputo 1993, 42–68.)

2 Corinthians 11:1–4

Zealous to Preserve Christ's Marriage Bed

The Text in Its Ancient Context

Here Paul raises the stakes on the church's flirtation with the super-apostles. He has married the Corinthians off to Christ; for them now to shift their allegiance to his rivals would be the same as abandoning their nuptial union with Christ. Paul makes a similar move in his letter to the Galatians (1:6–9), where a note similar to verse 4 can be heard.

The Text in the Interpretive Tradition

Paul, in unconscious cooperation with the Song of Songs, had perhaps no more profound influence on later doctrine than in the nuptial imagery he employs here for the relation of Christ and the church (for the early church, see Elliott; for a medieval example, see Gilbert of Hoyland, *Sermons* 2.5). Luther's notion of the "joyous exchange" comes out of this tradition (see, e.g., his *The Blessed Sacrament of the Holy and True Body of Christ and the Brotherhoods* [*LW* 35]).

The Text in Contemporary Discussion

Unlike their medieval counterparts, today's readers are no doubt bewildered or put off by the conceptual framework of Christ as bridegroom and the church as bride. To be sure, definite risks accompany this way of imagining Christian doctrine and piety. First of all, there appears to be a bias toward heterosexual marriage that abets heterosexism in contemporary culture (on which see Jung and Smith). To counter this impression that Paul is a champion of heterosexual marriage, one need only read his tepid commendation of marriage in 1 Thess. 4:3–8 and 1 Corinthians 7 (see Martin 2006). Moreover, nuptial imagery actually has the potential of deconstructing the binary opposition of male and female--think of Corinthian manbrides! (See Fredrickson 2013, 129–49). Finally, a clear distinction must be made between Paul's use of nuptial imagery in his genuine epistles and that found in the pseudonymous letters (Colossians, Ephesians, and the Pastorals). In the former, Paul emphasizes the ritual of marriage, the wedding, and does so in the context of eschatological expectation. Furthermore, standard motifs of friendship (the theme of *koinōnia*, for example) define what it means to get married. In the pseudonymous letters, however, marriage is placed within the ancient Greek household (see Balch) and illustrates the same hierarchical relation that obtains between head and body and Christ and church, the very relations of power and authority that the genuine Paul says Christ is presently nullifying (see 1 Cor. 15:24; for the brazen misconstrual of this verse to legitimate hierarchy, see Eph. 1:20–23).

2 Corinthians 11:5–12:10

Dog Apostles, Hardships, and Weakness

The Text in Its Ancient Context

As God is his witness, Paul loves the Corinthians (11:11). For that reason, they should take his refusal of financial support not as an insult but rather as witness of his affection. But there is more to his refusal than this. Paul is setting up an extended comparison between himself and the super-apostles in 11:12–12:13, just what he said in 10:12 he would not do. The comparison hinges on the opponents' Cynic-like behavior. In this connection, note in 11:9 that he refuses the Corinthians' aid in order that he might keep himself in every way "without weight" (*abarē*). The term "weighty" (*baros*) was often associated with Cynic philosophers (Malherbe 1970) whose harsh criticism was felt to be oppressive. Cynics also had the reputation of throwing their weight around in another way: by demanding lodging from the very people they rebuked. And then they ate them out of house and home (see 11:20: "preys upon you" might also be translated "eats up" or "devours"). Cynics, in short, had big jaws (see Billerbeck, 113).

Paul compliments himself perhaps too much (or is his sense of humor very dry?) when he explains the reason for this comparison with the super-apostles: he wants to prevent them from "being found as he is" (11:12). It turns out that Paul is a wreck, but before he enumerates his hardships (11:23–33) and exposes his weaknesses (12:8–10), he alludes in 11:13–15 and 20–21 to behavioral traits frequently associated with Cynic behavior. (The name "Cynic" is related to the Greek word for dog; for these traits, see Epictetus, *Diatr.* 2.12.24; 3.22.23–25, 45–50; 4.8.6–20; Lucian, *Fugitivi* 12–19; *Piscator* 31; Aelius Aristides, *Oration*

3.663–68, 671, 676, 682–83; Julian, *Oration* 6.201A.) He implies that the Corinthians ought to be horrified in discovering the super-apostles' real identity and ashamed not to have seen it before. Perhaps most important here is that the doglike apostles are portrayed as minions of Satan (11:14–15), whom we have encountered before in this letter when severity threatens to drive an individual through shame to suicide (2:5–11).

Ancient philosophers listed their hardships for three reasons: to display their moral virtue; to describe training in moral virtue; and, less frequently, to show their kindly attitude (*philanthrōpia*) toward the ignorant masses they sought to improve (see Fitzgerald). In 11:23–33, Paul mimics the philosopher's occupational hazards; but in verses 28–29 he slips in sentiments illustrative not of a moralist's day-to-day troubles but of the emotions of those who care for and fret over a beloved, even to the point of burning (cf. 1 Cor. 7:9).

Second Corinthians 12:1–10 is a tour de force in which Paul makes the following point, representative of the entire letter, by having the Lord himself say it (12:9): weakness—the lover's sickness of body and soul when separated from the beloved—perfects divine power. The Lord should know of what he speaks, since he was crucified "out of weakness" (13:4). But why, from first-century perspectives, does Paul stage the event of his abduction into paradise in such dramatic terms? It is not an overstatement to say that in the ancient Greek world, anyone who had something important to say, especially about the great transitions of individual or community life, what anthropologists call liminality, told a story of erotic abduction. Consider Homer's *Iliad*, the founding of Europe, Zeus's love for Ganymede, Eos's desire for Tithonos, the educational experience of the young men of Sparta and Crete, the tolerance of forced marriages by abduction, and the bitterly protested marriages to Hades at death. It is not unreasonable to suppose that Paul could not have told the most important story of his life and of his ministry without narrating rapture into paradise (for erotic abduction and sexual violence in ancient culture, see Fredrickson 2013, 85–104). But in this mysterious event, this apocalypse, he refuses to boast. Of course, by saying that he won't talk about it, he speaks volumes.

The Text in the Interpretive Tradition

The eroticism of these verses has faded from view in the modern period, but some readers, especially medieval mystics and monastics, experienced a reawakening of friendship in theology and in their communal life and treasured Paul's abduction (*harpagenta* in v. 2 and *hērpagē* in v. 4) into paradise, the unspeakable, wordless intimacy, and his disorienting and grief-filled return to earth. Paul's story matched their brief ecstasies and then the long and hollow periods of Christ's absence. There was a particular interest in Paul's experience of hearing "wordless words" (*arrēta rēmata*, 12:4), which was understood as erotic and an example of apophaticism (see John of Ford, *Sermons* 4.1; 45.2, 5; 94.9; 100.5).

The Text in Contemporary Discussion

Apophaticism, or negative theology, is a kind of theological discourse that denies, inconsistently, that it is possible to speak about God. God is beyond being, it is claimed, and therefore to speak about God violates God, and yet this very impossibility impassions more and more words spoken and written about God. Robust in the medieval period, when Paul's loquacious silence about his encounter with Jesus in 2 Cor. 12:4 served as a kind of proof text, apophaticism is making a comeback in postmodern philosophy and theology thanks to the fascination the contradiction between speaking and not speaking held for Jacques Derrida. Derrida did not, however, share negative theology's confidence that it could *rest* in the God beyond being, beyond linguistic signification. Quite the opposite. In an uncanny and certainly unintended parallel to Paul's return to earth (12:7–10), where divine power happens in weakness, that is, in Paul's troubled, loving relation to the Corinthians, Derrida generalized the impossibility and passion of the speaking about God to the speaking about every other. "Deconstruction is rather the thought, if it is a thought, of an absolute heterogeneity that unsettles all the assurances of the same within which we comfortably ensconce ourselves. That is the desire by which it is moved, which moves and impassions it, which sets it into motion, toward which it extends itself" (Caputo 1997, 5).

2 Corinthians 12:11–13:10

A True Apostle

The Text in Its Ancient Context

The letter is coming to an end. Paul must first extricate himself from his pretense of boasting and comparison with the super-apostles. This he accomplishes in 12:11–13 by shifting blame: the Corinthians themselves forced him to act the part of a bragging fool.

In 12:13–15, he deals one last time with the implications of his refusal of financial support. First, he seeks (the Greek term *zēteō* has erotic connotations and might also be translated "desires") them, not their things. Second, he is their parent (cf. 1 Cor. 4:14–15). The last reason (v. 15) can of course be read in terms of economics, but the words carry an erotic connotation as well, which should not be unexpected given the emphasis on love at the end of the verse. The words in question here are *dapanaō* and *ekdapanaō* (NRSV: "spend and be spent"). The first term might reasonably carry only economic meaning, but the fact that the second is used in the passive voice means that Paul himself is expended for their lives. There is continuity with the motif of *servitium amoris* running throughout the letter. Two obvious parallels are 1 Thess. 2:8 and Phil. 2:17. A more subtle parallel is Phil. 2:7, in which Christ is said to have "emptied himself." In Greek and Latin love literature, longing for communion with a beloved causes the lover to melt and then drain away, in other words to be poured out or expended (see Fredrickson 2013, 45–83; for a much later example of *dapanaō* used in this erotic sense, see Theodorus Prodromus, *Rhodanthe and Dosicles* 8.179: "the hearts of those who long are expended").

Before he bids farewell in a proto-trinitarian formula (13:13), which is itself significant in its repetition of Paul's emphasis throughout the letter on love, grace, and communion, Paul concludes the body of the letter with three final contrasts between himself and the super-apostles. First, in 12:20, as he returns to the ethical and social class issues he had addressed in 1 Corinthians (likely linked through elite male privileges), Paul makes a surprising turn: the church's bad behavior will be the occasion of God driving him once again into melancholy and causing him to lament. Reading verse 21 first and then going back to the first half of verse 20 raises a question: Is Paul suggesting that their finding him "not as they wish" means that they will find him weak and lacking in the severity of the super-apostles? Second Corinthians 13:3 hints that this was the case. The second contrast is the oblique criticism in 13:5–10 that Paul's rivals engage in moral exhortation in order to burnish their own reputations for frank speaking. Paul claims to have no stake in the Corinthians' progress other than their improvement. The final contrast, which ends the body of the letter, has Paul locating the purpose of his authority not in harsh criticism (the Greek phrase connotes "cutting") but in building up.

The Text in the Interpretive Tradition

In a stunning turn, the very weakness (*asthenia*) Paul seeks mightily to preserve in the face of the super-apostles' harshness, even to the point of his adopting the guise of a warrior, became an embarrassment to the apostle's later interpreters. But Paul plainly *does* connect his weakness to Christ's in 13:4: "he [Christ] was crucified from weakness" and "we are weak in him." The subtle adjustments made to the first phrase by exegetes betray their nervousness over its dogmatic implication that weakness pertains to the whole Christ, a view that the fathers worried the uneducated reader might erroneously entertain (John Chrysostom, *In epistulam ii ad Corinthos* [PG 61:598–600]).

One solution to the perceived threat to the *apatheia* of God, a nonnegotiable point in Christian theology as soon as ancient philosophy was let in, was to assign the weakness mentioned in 13:4 to Christ's "human part" or "nature" or to his "flesh." His resurrection, power, and life were referred to the divine (see Gregory of Nyssa, *Contra Eunomium* 3.4.10). A related strategy was to deny any passivity in Christ. In Eusebius's words, "He himself made himself weak, not being conquered by another" (*Commentaria in Psalmos* 23.309). Christ's *voluntary* weakness made it not weakness in the usual sense (see Cyril of Jerusalem,

Catacheses ad illuminandos 14.8). Finally, weakness might be understood simply as a matter of suffering persecution or plots (see John of Damascus, *Commentarii in epistulas Pauli* [PG 95:773).

The Text in Contemporary Discussion

Second Corinthians begins (1:3) and ends (13:4) with divine suffering. The interpretive tradition's discomfort with Paul's straying outside the lines drawn for theology by the doctrine of the *apatheia* of God, a doctrine inspired by Greek philosophy, make Paul's weakness, his passions, all the more interesting. On several occasions in this essay, it was pointed out that Paul's subtle use and critique of Greek philosophical ideas make his writings a site of exploration for postmodern philosophers, especially those, like John Caputo, influenced by Jacques Derrida.

If we shift from God to Paul, a distinction that Paul himself obscures throughout the letter (see, e.g., 5:20–21), we note that the interpretive tradition generally characterized Paul's suffering as his endurance of hardships or opposition not unlike the wise man's training in virtue. Yet here are good reasons to think that his suffering was in fact the vulnerability opened up in him by loving the Corinthians: weakness, in other words. We have seen that Paul aligns himself with the weakness of Christ, and this leads him to a pastoral practice of adaptability, grace, and forgiveness, none of which compromises frank speech from Paul's perspective, as the harsh super-apostles charge, but that works in concert with truth-telling and justice. Paul insists on the "slavery of love" (*servitium amoris*) and related motifs drawn from erotic literature to unify the argument of the letter and persuade the Corinthians to accept his ministry and to reject that of his rivals. Finally, we observed how the letter's critique of the severe disciplinary practice that had the effect of isolating the individual who wronged Paul challenges the contemporary church to examine its understanding of punishment and the isolating practices of the American system of criminal justice.

WORKS CITED

Amador, J. D. H. 2000. "Revisiting 2 Corinthians: Rhetoric and the Case for Unity." *NTS* 46:92–111.

Balch, David L. 1981. *Let Wives Be Submissive: The Domestic Code in 1 Peter.* SBLMS 26. Chico, CA: Scholars Press.

Barrett, C. K. 1970. "Ο ΑΔΙΚΗΣΑΣ (2 Cor. 7.12)." In *Verborum Veritas: Festschrift für Gustav Stählin*, edited by Otto Böcher and Klaus Haacker, 149–57. Wuppertal: Rolf Brockhaus.

Barrett, C. K. 1973. *A Commentary on the Second Epistle to the Corinthians.* HNTC. New York: Harper & Row.

Barth, Karl. 2002. *The Epistle to the Philippians.* Translated by James W. Leitch. 40th anniversary ed. Louisville: Westminster John Knox.

Betz, Hans Dieter, and George W. MacCrae. 1985. *2 Corinthians 8 and 9: A Commentary on Two Administrative Letters of the Apostle Paul.* Philadelphia: Fortress Press.

Billerbeck, Margarethe. 1978. *Epiktet: Vom Kynismus.* Philosophia Antiqua 34. Leiden: Brill.

Briggs, Sheila. 1989. "Can an Enslaved God Liberate? Hermeneutical Reflections on Phil 2:6–11." *Semeia* 47:137–53.

Caputo, John D. 1993. *Against Ethics: Contributions to a Poetics of Obligation with Constant Reference to Deconstruction.* Bloomington: Indiana University Press.

Caputo, John D. 1997. *The Prayers and Tears of Jacques Derrida: Religion without Religion.* Bloomington: Indiana University Press.

Caputo, John D., and Linda Martin Alcoff. 2009. *St. Paul among the Philosophers.* Bloomington: Indiana University Press.

Culler, Jonathan D. 1982. *On Deconstruction: Theory and Criticism after Structuralism.* Ithaca, NY: Cornell University Press.

Danker, Frederick W. 1982. *Benefactor: An Epigraphic Study of a Graeco-Roman and New Testament Semantic Field.* Saint Louis: Clayton.

Derrida, Jacques. 2005. *The Politics of Friendship.* New York: Verso.

Elliott, M. W. 2000. *The Song of Songs and Christology in the Early Church, 381–451*. Studien und Texte zu Antike und Christentum 7. Tübingen: Mohr Siebeck.

Fitzgerald, John T. 1988. *Cracks in an Earthen Vessel: An Examination of the Catalogues of Hardships in the Corinthian Correspondence*. SBLDS 99. Atlanta: Scholars Press.

Fiore, Benjamin. 1985. "'Covert Allusion' in 1 Corinthians 1–4." *CBQ* 47:85–102.

Fredrickson, David E. 1996. "*Parrēsia* in the Pauline Epistles." In *Friendship, Flattery, and Frankness of Speech: Studies on Friendship in the New Testament World*, edited by John T. Fitzgerald, 163–84. NovTSup 82. New York: Brill.

Fredrickson, David E. 1997. "The Presence of Jesus in 2 Corinthians 1-7." In *The Quest for Jesus and the Christian Faith*, edited by Frederick J. Gaiser, 163–74. Word and World Supplements 3. St. Paul: Word and World.

Fredrickson, David E. 2000. "Paul's Sentence of Death (2 Corinthians 1:9)." In *God, Evil, and Suffering: Essays in Honor of Paul R. Sponheim*, edited by Terence E. Fretheim and Curtis L. Thompson, 99–107. Word and World Supplements 4. St. Paul: Word and World.

Fredrickson, David E. 2001. "'Through Many Tears (2 Cor 2:4)': Paul's Grieving Letter and the Occasion of 2 Corinthians 1–7." In *Paul and Pathos*, edited by Thomas H. Olbricht and Jerry L. Sumney, 161–79. Atlanta: Society of Biblical Literature.

Fredrickson, David E. 2013. *Eros and the Christ: Longing and Envy in Paul's Christology*. Minneapolis: Fortress Press.

Fretheim, Terence E. 1984. *The Suffering of God: An Old Testament Perspective*. OBT 14. Philadelphia: Fortress Press.

Frick, Peter, ed. 2013. *Paul in the Grip of the Philosophers: The Apostle and Contemporary Continental Philosophy*. Minneapolis: Fortress Press.

Furnish, Victor Paul. 1984. *2 Corinthians*. AB. Garden City, NY: Doubleday.

Georgi, Dieter. 1987. *The Opponents of Paul in Second Corinthians*. Studies of the New Testament and its World. Edinburgh: T&T Clark.

Grant, Robert M. 1957. *The Letter and the Spirit*. London: SPCK.

Horner, Robyn. 2001. *Rethinking God as Gift: Marion, Derrida, and the Limits of Phenomenology*. Perspectives in Continental Philosophy 19. New York: Fordham University Press.

Kearney, Richard. 2005. "Deconstruction, God, and the Possible." In *Derrida and Religion: Other Testaments*, edited by Yvonne Sherwood and Kevin Hart, 297–308. New York: Routledge.

Jung, Patricia B., and Ralph F. Smith. 1993. *Heterosexism: An Ethical Challenge*. Albany: State University of New York Press.

Malherbe, Abraham J. 1970. " 'Gentle as a Nurse': The Cynic Background to I Thess II." *NovT* 12:203–17.

Malherbe, Abraham J. 1983. "Exhortation in First Thessalonians." *NovT* 25:238–56.

Malherbe, Abraham J. 1988. *Ancient Epistolary Theorists*. SBLSBS 19. Atlanta: Scholars Press.

Malherbe, Abraham J. 1989. *Paul and the Popular Philosophers*. Minneapolis: Augsburg Fortress.

Marshall, Peter. 1987. *Enmity in Corinth: Social Conventions in Paul's Relations with the Corinthians*. WUNT 23. Tübingen: J. C. B. Mohr.

Martin, Dale B. 1990. *Slavery as Salvation: The Metaphor of Slavery in Pauline Christianity*. New Haven: Yale University Press.

Martin, Dale B. 2006. *Sex and the Single Savior: Gender and Sexuality in Biblical Interpretation*. Louisville: Westminster John Knox.

McGinn, Bernard. 1996. "God as Eros: Metaphysical Foundations of Christian Mysticism." In *New Perspectives on Historical Theology: Essays in Memory of John Meyendorff*, edited by Bradley Nassif, 189–209. Grand Rapids: Eerdmans.

Miller, John F. 1995. "Reading Cupid's Triumph." *Classical Journal* 90:287–94.

Mitchell, Margaret. 2002. *The Heavenly Trumpet: John Chrysostom and the Art of Pauline Interpretation*. HUT 40. Louisville: Westminster John Knox.

Moltmann, Jürgen. 1974. *The Crucified God: The Cross of Christ as the Foundation and Criticism of Christian Theology*. New York: Harper & Row.

Moltmann, Jürgen. 1981. *The Trinity and the Kingdom: The Doctrine of God*. San Francisco: Harper & Row.

Monks of Mount Saint Bernard Abbey. 1970–1971. *Guerric of Igny: Liturgical Sermons*. 2 vols. Cistercian Fathers 8, 32. Spencer, MA: Cistercian.

Murgatroyd, Paul. 1980. "*Servitium Amoris* and the Roman Elegists." *Latomus* 40:589–606.

Nietzsche, Friedrich. 1998. *On the Genealogy of Morality: A Polemic*. Translated by Maudemarie Clark and Alan J. Swensen. Indianapolis: Hackett.

Smiley, Charles Newton. 1906. *Latinitas and Hellēnismos: The Influence of the Stoic Theory of Style as Shown in the Writings of Dionysius, Quintilian, Pliny the Younger, Tacitus, Fronto, Aulus Gellius, and Sextus Empiricus*. Madison: University of Wisconsin.

Schmithals, Walter. 1971. *Gnosticism in Corinth: An Investigation of the Letters to the Corinthians*. Nashville: Abingdon.

Stowers, Stanley K. 1986. *Letter Writing in Greco-Roman Antiquity*. LEC 5. Philadelphia: Westminster.

Van Hook, Larue. 1905. *The Metaphorical Terminology of Greek Rhetoric and Literary Criticism*. Chicago: University of Chicago Press.

Voit, Ludwig. 1934. ΔΕΙΝΟΤΗΣ: *Ein antiker Stilbegriff*. Leipzig: Dieterich.

Walters, Gregory. 2013. *Being Promised: Theology, Gift, and Practice*. Sacra Doctrina. Grand Rapids: Eerdmans.

Watson, Francis B. 1984. "2 Cor. X–XIII and Paul's Painful Letter to the Corinthians." *JTS* 35:324–46.

Zagagi, Netta.1980. *Tradition and Originality in Plautus: Studies in the Amatory Motif in Plautine Comedy*. Hypomnemata 62. Göttingen: Vandenhoeck & Ruprecht.